W9-DFK-892

# Once Upon a Tree

# Once Upon a Tree

## *Life from Treetop to Root Tips*

*Written and Illustrated by* James B. Nardi

*Iowa State University Press / Ames*

James B. Nardi received his Ph.D. degree from Harvard University and is now research scientist, Department of Entomology, University of Illinois. Since childhood, his fascination with the natural world, particularly insects, has enhanced his appreciation of living systems and guided the course of his life. He is also author of *Close Encounters with Insects and Spiders,* published by Iowa State University Press.



♾ Printed on acid-free paper in the United States of America

First edition, 1993

---

Library of Congress Cataloging-in-Publication Data
Nardi, James B.
Once upon a tree : life from treetop to root tips / written and illustrated by James B. Nardi. – 1st ed.
p. cm.
Includes index.
Summary: Examines the diverse life one can find on a tree and relates how the various plants and animals coexist.
ISBN 0-8138-0917-7 (acid-free paper)
1. Forest ecology – Juvenile literature. [1. Forest ecology. 2. Trees. 3. Ecology.] I. Title.
QH541.5.F6N37 1993
574.5′2642 – dc20 92-36444

# CONTENTS

A great crested flycatcher chasing a tree hole midge.

Every tree has a unique and interesting story to tell about the life forms associated with it.

# PREFACE

You can tell a lot about trees from the company they keep. Whether they live in the tropics or in the north woods, the creatures that depend on trees always have certain jobs to perform. Each tree community has its prey and predators, its decomposers and recyclers, its planters and harvesters. Trees and the creatures of these communities may be different from place to place, but their jobs are more or less the same everywhere. This book emphasizes this rich diversity and interplay of life on a tree, from treetop to root tips.

The creatures mentioned in this book happen to be those that you are likely to encounter on a walk or while gazing out your windows. Some creatures will already be familiar to a number of you, but others will look and sound extraordinary. Believe me, they really do exist on trees, and if you are a patient observer, you will very likely find them.

Life in a tree community is so rich that only representatives of major groups of animals and plants are discussed and illustrated on the pages that follow. Ideas are presented for activities that can help you learn more from trees by introducing you to a number of the creatures found between the treetops and root tips. The intent of this book is not to be comprehensive but to arouse your curiosity, stimulate additional inquiries, and encourage some closer looks at life in the tree communities. And maybe some new discoveries will be made along the way too.

The story told by every tree changes with the seasons.

# ACKNOWLEDGMENTS

By interacting with friends and colleagues in our own communities, we enhance our lives and our activities. I am grateful to all those whose generous help and enthusiasm have left their marks on this book.

In the farm community where I grew up, trees of an orchard and forest were some of our nearest neighbors. By introducing me to the trees of the farm and the companions of the trees, my parents gave me a gift that has never lost its allure.

What began as observations, notes, and sketches from my encounters with trees evolved into text and illustrations for this book. Other ideas developed as friends brought me creatures they had found on trees. A friend who lives in the country, Susan Gabay-Laughnan, kept a sharp lookout for insects that live in trees. Thanks to her, several moths and the horntail are included in this book. Janet Day, who spends many hours in the field, brought me many insects she had found. One spring morning David Bergstrom presented me with a treehopper nymph that I had never seen before.

My colleagues who study insects and plants gladly shared their knowledge and experiences with me. I spent many pleasant hours with Ellis MacLeod, discussing the ways of insects and learning from an excellent teacher. From David Voegtlin I learned more about the strange lives of aphids, and thanks to George Godfrey, I learned more about certain moths that live with trees. Ken Robertson and Larry Hoffman helped me understand some confusing features of flowers that are found on trees.

Almut Jones, who is curator of the University of Illinois Herbarium, loaned me specimens of plants and shared stories of trees with me. The staff at the Museum of Natural History at the University of Illinois helped me find study skins of birds and mammals that I wanted to examine. Kathleen Methven and Kathryn McGiffen at the Illinois Natural History Survey located insect specimens in the survey's collection that I needed to study for certain illustrations.

My two friends who are artists, Jackie Worden and Mary Swope, provided the advice and encouragement I often needed during the long hours I spent illustrating the text.

Catherine Birdseye offered to proofread the first handwritten draft of the manuscript. Her critical eye was responsible for many improvements. Lorie Hatfield typed the manuscript, sparing me that painful task.

The staff at the Iowa State University Press, Lynne Bishop, Bob Campbell, and Kathy Walker, patiently and skillfully dealt with editing and production.

Some of the trees and creatures that I studied and admired during the preparation of this book would not have existed without the concern of certain caring people. I thank all those people who have saved trees and who have planted trees for making our earth a richer and lovelier place.

# Once Upon a Tree

Web of interactions in a tree community. By following the arrows in the food web, you can trace the flow of nutrients through the tree community.

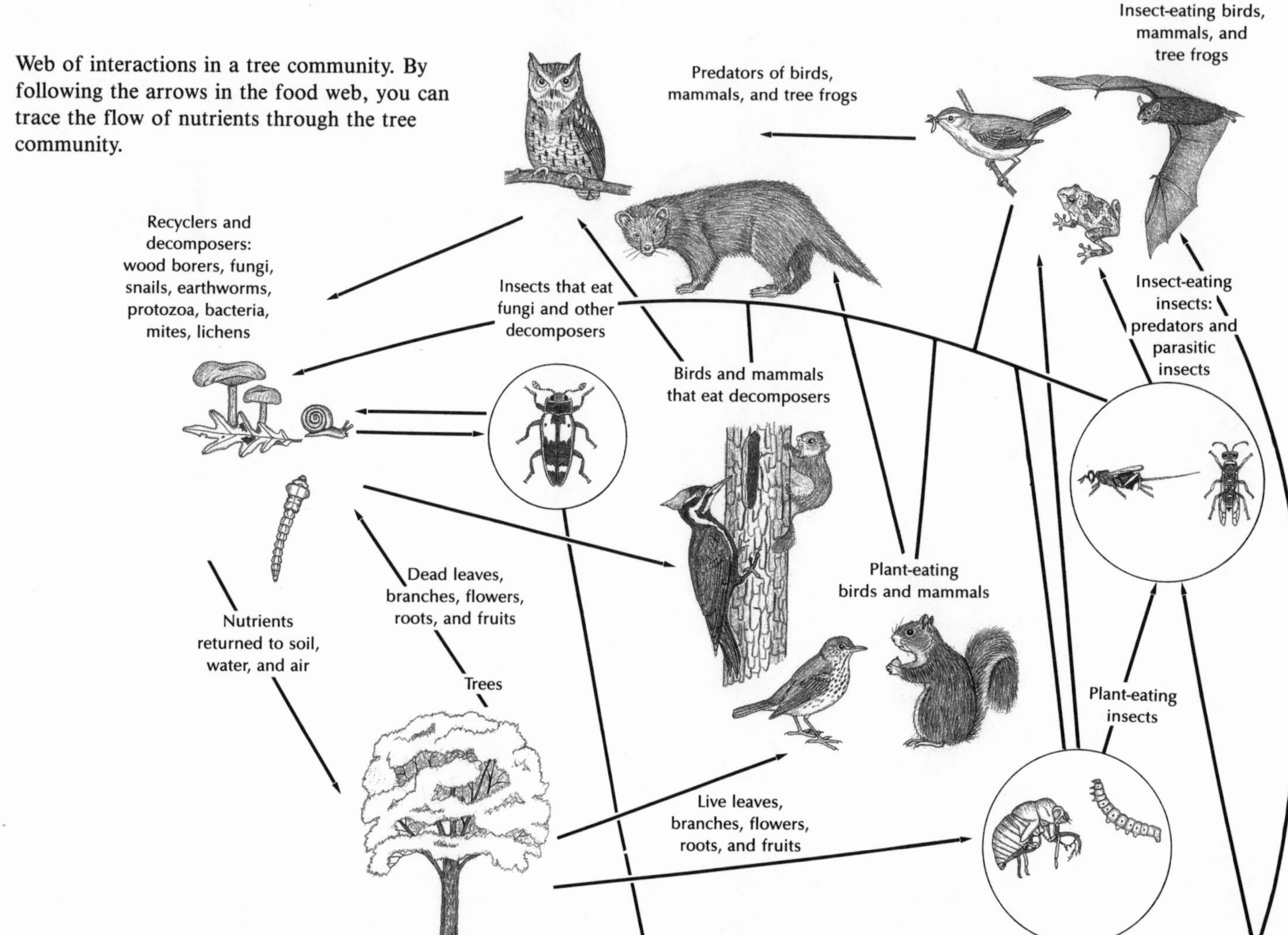

# The Intricate Web

All things are connected like the blood that unites us. We did not weave this web of life. We are merely a strand in it. Whatever we do to the web, we do to ourselves.

Chief Seattle

We frequently are told by those with little imagination that the last frontiers have been explored on our small planet and that we should look to the heavens for our next new frontiers. But our gazes toward the heavens do not need to wander beyond the trees that we pass every day. New frontiers lie as near as the closest trees that stretch from the earth toward the sky.

From treetop to root tips, wherever trees grow, each tree hosts its own community of creatures. Some creatures choose a particular tree for its fruits or leaves; others are attracted by its hollow limbs or insect life. Each creature seems to find what it needs somewhere on the tree and always manages to repay the tree in some way for its generosity.

Every tree, whether it is rooted in a great forest, city park, or backyard, has a unique and interesting story to tell about the creatures that are associated with it. If someone ever counted all the different forms of life that inhabit a tree and draw their strength from a tree, that number would be a great surprise to most of us. Not many people realize just how many life forms dwell unseen among the leaves and branches above our heads as well as on the roots beneath our feet. We can study the interdependence of these lives without ever looking farther afield than the tree outside our window. By observing carefully, some surprising discoveries can come our way.

Looking closely at a tree reveals that it is a busy crossroads of activity where innumerable lives arrive, depart, or just carry on. The closer we inspect any part of a tree, the more creatures we find and the more we discover how their relationships are woven together. We can think of each tree as a community where creatures are caught in a web of interactions that links them to each other and to the tree in which they live. This web of interactions involves cooperation, coexistence, and competition among members of the community. And even though individual animals may fall prey to their predators and entire trees may have their leaves devoured, the members of the web manage to transact their business—giving and taking—and usually balance their accounts so that few, if any, species gain or lose too much. Each species has its job to do and does it. One tree can thus support—directly or indirectly—many lives.

The partnership between trees and other creatures has been a very successful one, probably because it is

Fox squirrel seeking shade on a walnut limb.

based more on cooperation than on competition. Long before humans appeared on earth, green plants, with the help of sunshine and chlorophyll, began the process that would produce nourishment and oxygen for themselves and for the creatures that share the earth with them. The process is known as photosynthesis, a word that means "to put together with light." Sugars and oxygen are "put together" from raw materials such as water from the soil and carbon dioxide from the air, using the energy that comes from sunlight. Chlorophyll is the green pigment in leaves that captures this energy of the sunlight. The energy is not lost in the process but is transferred to the sugars that the tree produces and then to the creatures that feed on the tree. Each life form uses energy to survive. When one creature eats another or eats a plant, it obtains energy from the meal. This is true whether that meal is alive or dead, plant or animal, or fungus. The tree is the only life form in the web that does not obtain its energy from another member of the community. All its energy comes from sunlight. Energy is constantly exchanged in the food web except for what is lost along the way as heat. Heat is generated by every living form, but all energy originally comes from sunlight and photosynthesis. Thus, photosynthesis not only provides the energy and oxygen for the other members of a tree community, but it also helps clear the air of carbon dioxide produced by all creatures as well as by fires, volcanoes, and engines. Can you see why trees and other green vegetation are so important for the survival of all creatures?

We often take for granted the many other gifts of trees. Trees muffle noises as well as add cheer and beauty to a landscape. They hold moisture in the soil, and they also protect the soil from eroding. With their roots, trees pull up nutrients from deep in the soil that will be shared with other creatures in their communities. Trees do not use all these nutrients during their growing season. Each year when they shed their leaves, trees return many of these nutrients to the earth to replenish the fertility of the land. Trees offer nourishment and refuge to people and animals alike. In the heat of summer, they provide coolness and shade. In the cold of winter, they block the icy winds. Who can doubt that by saving trees and planting more trees, we are investing in the integrity and beauty of the earth?

For better or for worse, we too are part of the community of a tree. We build homes, boats, and furniture with wood. The paper we write on and use to make books, paper bags, and cardboard boxes are made from trees. We cultivate soils that were enriched for centuries by the decay of billions of leaves and animals that once lived on trees. Our stores are filled with fruits, nuts, and honey harvested from trees in orchards and forests around the world. We burn wood in our fireplaces and campfires, and we breathe air that has been cleansed by the leaves. The community of life associated with a tree eventually suffers if our relationship with it is one of constantly taking gifts and never giving in return. Ultimately we too suffer from our thoughtlessness.

Our relationships with trees have posed many questions throughout history, and more questions are posed now than at any previous time about our stewardship of trees and the earth. A few questions raise many issues about our values and ultimately about our destiny. How many trees can we save by recycling paper bags, cardboard, and newspapers or by not using paper bags for shopping? How many trees should be sacrificed to make room for a shopping mall, a highway, or a new housing subdivision? Should rows of trees be preserved between farm fields as havens for wildlife or removed to enhance the efficiency of our farming? How many trees should be cleared in the forests of Latin America

A tree sparrow sheltered by spruce branches.

to raise beef cattle for fast-food restaurants? How many majestic trees in the world's rain forests should be cut to satisfy our ever-growing hunger for lumber?

As the trees disappear, so will many of the birds, insects, and other animals that depend on trees for their well-being. We are already seeing declines in the populations of our songbirds, some to the point of extinction. Many of the smaller creatures of trees may also be disappearing, but we are unaware of their plight. How will the disappearance of trees and forests and animals affect our own well-being?

The history of our relationships with trees is filled with sad and thoughtless acts, but we can still learn to be wiser stewards by studying the examples of creatures that live in harmony with the trees. Many of their stories are told on the pages that follow.

# LEARNING FROM TREES

Strange that so few ever come into the woods to see how the pine lives and grows and spires, lifting its evergreen arms to the light—to see its perfect success; but most are content to behold it in the shape of many broad boards brought to market, and deem that its true success.

HENRY DAVID THOREAU

Trees are givers of knowledge as well as givers of lumber, shade, and fruit. This knowledge is given to those who patiently observe; and because it must be earned in this way, it is a gift to be especially cherished. There are many roads to knowledge and many ways to observe.

Finding many of the creatures on a tree is not hard. Try adopting a neighborhood tree. Examine its bark, leaves, flowers, and fruits for a few minutes each day over a period of a week, a month, or even a year. Look for birds and squirrels with binoculars. Hornet nests and woodpecker holes are also easy to spot. But other creatures of the tree are not as easy to find. To find some of them you will have to be clever, patient, and even lucky. If your tree could talk, what tales it would tell. Trees, like people, are individuals and each has unique tales to tell about the many lives that pass by or the lives that meet and linger beneath its branches and among its leaves.

Making observations from a tree house will give you a very different perspective about what happens on a tree. Not only is a tree house fun to build, but if it is well hidden, it will also give you a window on a world that is rarely seen from the ground. From your hidden perch you will meet birds, insects, and even frogs that spend most of their days high aboveground. And you may also see animals like raccoons, squirrels, and porcupines that come and go between the treetop and the ground.



# Flowers, Bees, and Trees

On a walk through the woods on a spring day, you may see carpets of wildflowers covering the ground, but you may not notice other flowers that are blooming on branches overhead. The first buds to open and the first colors to appear on many trees are those of their flowers. Some of these early flowers may be tiny and easily overlooked, but others have unmistakable colors, scents, and shapes. Orange, red, or yellow flowers adorn the branches of elms and maples many days before their first leaves appear. On oaks, apples, and willows, flowers and leaves unfold at the same time. But the fragrant flowers of tulip trees, wild cherries, and

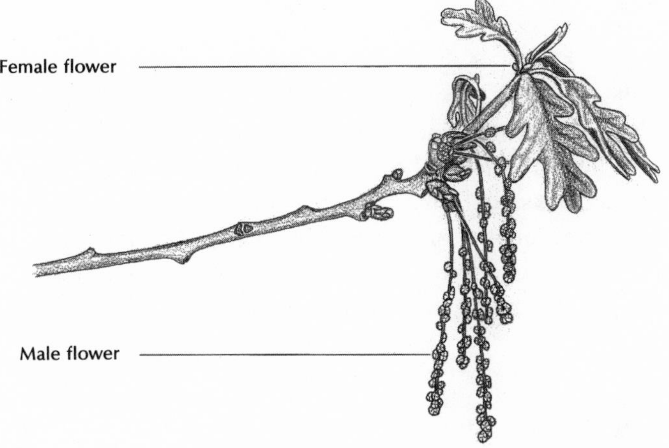


White oaks have separate male and female flowers that open at the same time that the leaves appear.

basswoods do not open until after their leaves are fully formed.

Each spring the flowers that bloom overhead join forces with insects and wind to bring about the process known as pollination. Without pollination of their flowers, trees cannot produce seeds and fruits. With the help of insects or wind, pollination occurs when pollen grains from the male anthers of stamens are transferred to the female stigmas of pistils. After landing on a stigma, a pollen grain sends forth a tube that grows down through the pistil until it reaches an ovule at the base of that pistil. The joining of pollen and an ovule produces a seed, and the surrounding cells of the ovary produce a fruit. Some fruits have only one seed, some have many seeds.

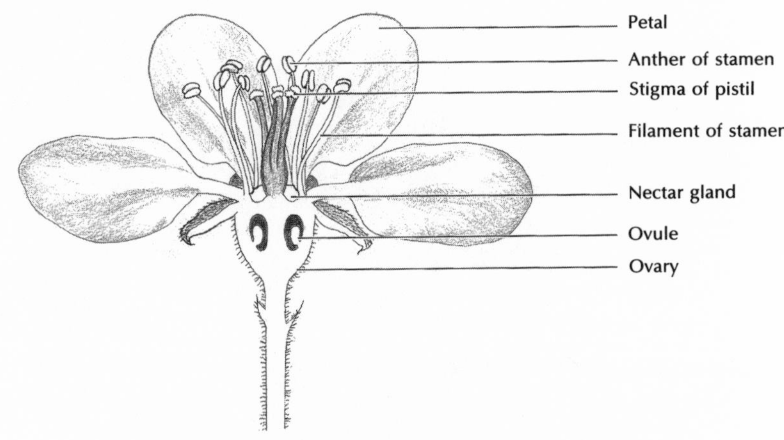


The major parts of a flower are shown in this cross section of an apple blossom.

The flowers of trees come in a variety of arrangements. Stamens and pistils may be found in the same flower, or they may be found either in separate flowers on the same tree or in separate flowers on different trees. Flowers having only stamens and anthers are known as staminate or male flowers. Flowers having only pistils are known as pistillate or female flowers. Whatever the arrangement of flowers on a tree, pollen grains somehow find their way to the pistils.

Wind carries the pollen of many trees like the pines, oaks, and elms. You may never have noticed their flowers, for they are neither showy nor fragrant. These trees are extravagant with their pollen, and on a windy day in the spring, clouds of pollen fill the air as they are

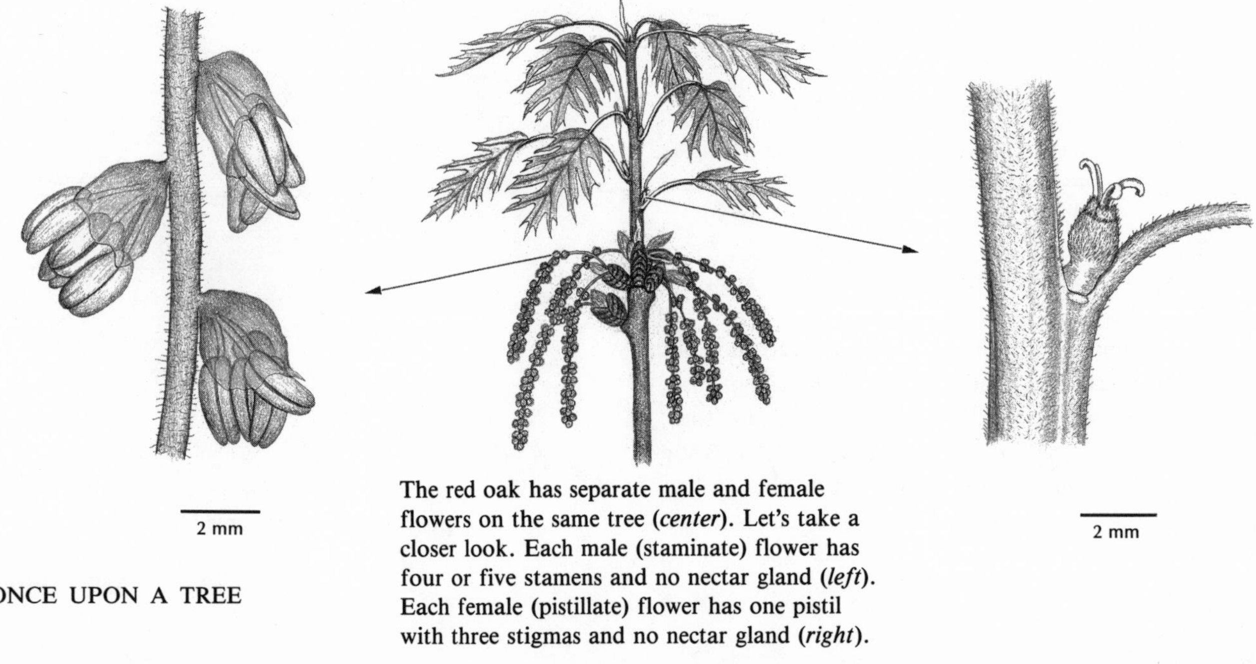


The red oak has separate male and female flowers on the same tree (*center*). Let's take a closer look. Each male (staminate) flower has four or five stamens and no nectar gland (*left*). Each female (pistillate) flower has one pistil with three stigmas and no nectar gland (*right*).

blown from tree to tree. Most of the pollen grains will never reach a pistil of another flower and will settle to the earth, but enough will still land on pistils of appropriate flowers to ensure a good crop of pine nuts, acorns, and elm fruits. These trees and others like birch, hickory, and walnut never rely on insects to pollinate their flowers—the wind is the main carrier of their pollen.

Trees like apple, cherry, catalpa, and willow have flowers that are fragrant or colorful or both fragrant and colorful, with sweet nectar and protein-rich pollen to attract insects that carry the pollen to their pistils. Insect-pollinated flowers store nectar in special glands at the base of each flower, and their pollen is generally stickier than pollen of wind-pollinated flowers. In their search for nectar, the insects usually get well dusted with the sticky pollen, which clings to them as they brush against it. The insects do a thorough job of visiting these flowers and transporting their pollen. Depending on pollination by insects is less chancy than depending on breezes that shift from day to day. Thus, insect-pollinated trees do not need to invest nearly as much energy in producing pollen as do wind-pollinated trees. However, even the insect-pollinated flowers produce large numbers of pollen grains. A single apple flower may produce 70,000 grains of pollen even though only ten of those grains are needed to produce the ten seeds of an apple. There is obviously a good supply of pollen remaining for the insect visitors.

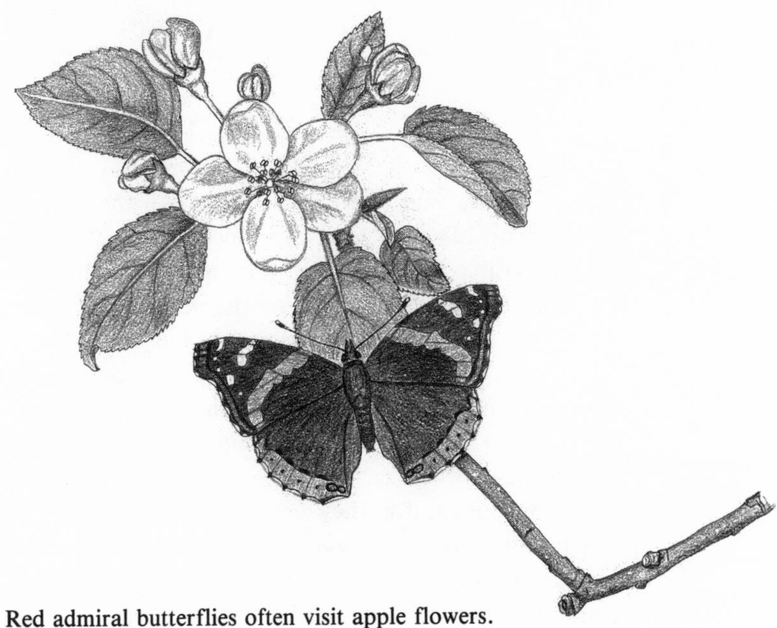

Red admiral butterflies often visit apple flowers.

Foraging honey bee seeking pollen and nectar (*top*). Honey bee with pollen baskets full (*bottom*).

Many insects such as beetles, flower flies, wasps, and butterflies visit flowers and help with the task of pollination while they search for nectar. However, bees are responsible for most of the pollinating. And unlike the other insects, bees forage on the nectar and collect the pollen, not only to feed themselves but also to stock their nests. The pollen and partially digested nectar (also known as honey) are stored in special compartments in the hive and are used as needed to feed adults and developing larvae. Honey bees are well suited for gathering pollen, for they are covered with hairs to which pollen clings. They even have special combs and brushes on their legs for combing the pollen from the hairs into "baskets" on their hind legs.

In the early spring, foraging honey bees fill the pollen baskets with pollen from willow flowers. These flowers happen to be some of the first flowers of the year. They might not be particularly attractive to our eyes or noses, but to bees that have neither seen nor smelled flowers for several months, their nectar and pollen have a strong appeal. After returning to their colony in some hollow tree or artificial hive box, the bees unload the pollen and nectar that they have harvested, restocking the honeycombs whose stores were emptied during the winter.

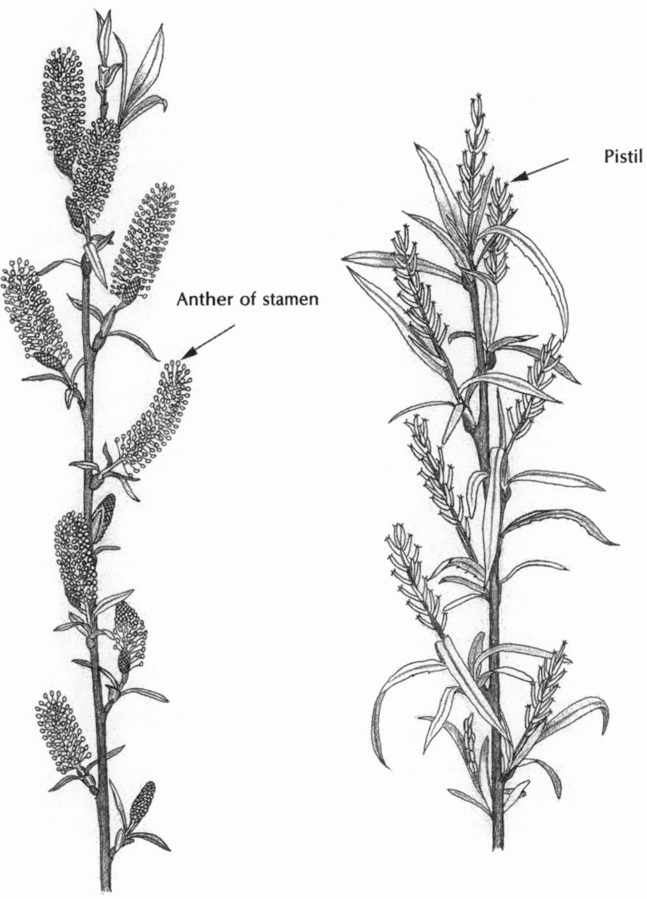


Willows have the male and female flowers on separate trees. Male flowers (*left*) of some species of willow are recognizable as the familiar "pussy." The female flowers (*right*) are not particularly attractive but produce some of the first spring nectar so appealing to foraging bees.

Willows happen to have male and female flowers on separate trees. Male flowers have both pollen and nectar to attract insects. Female flowers have only nectar to offer, but they also attract their share of insects. Female flowers must have some attraction to offer the bees, otherwise they would visit only the male flowers and pollination would never take place. Any number of arrangements of male and female flowers is apparently acceptable to insects as long as they are rewarded in some way for visiting a flower.

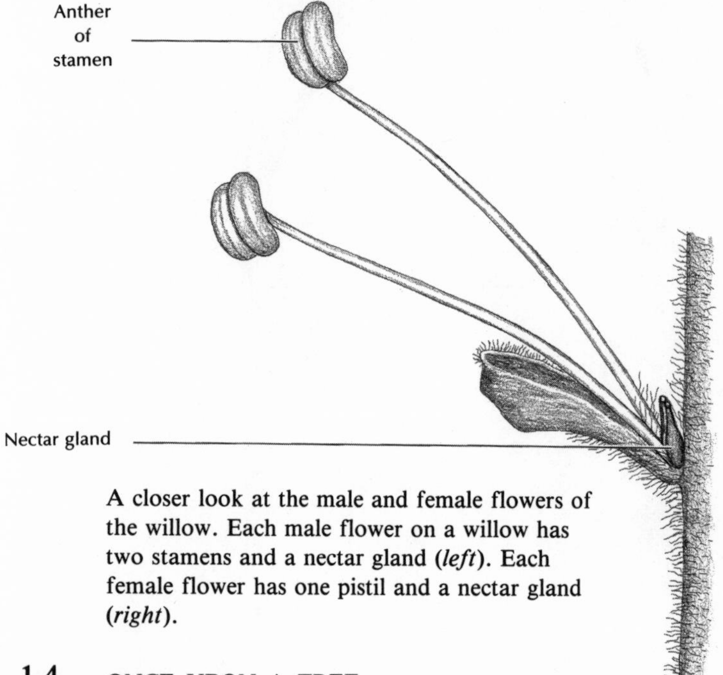


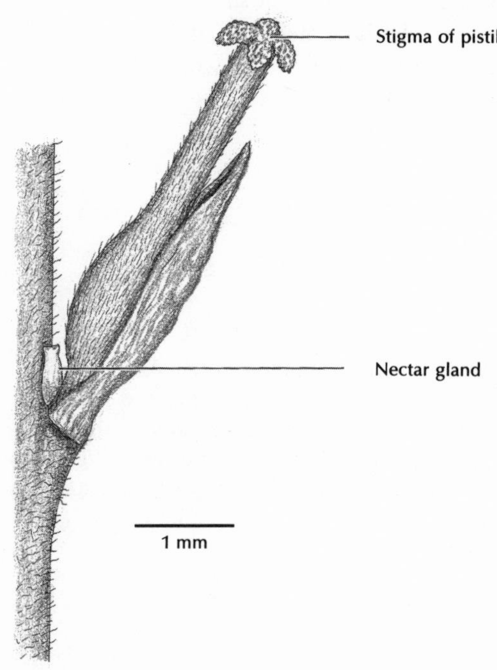


A closer look at the male and female flowers of the willow. Each male flower on a willow has two stamens and a nectar gland (*left*). Each female flower has one pistil and a nectar gland (*right*).

Hold your palm under the flower of a tree and tap the flower with your other hand. If the flower has mature pollen, your palm will be dusted with hundreds or thousands of pollen grains. Notice how the pollen of some trees is stickier than that of other trees. Does pollen come in more than one color and size? Look at some pollen under a microscope or magnifying lens. Magnification will reveal that the pollen of each tree has its own distinctive shape and sculpturing.

A person experienced at examining pollen grains is called a palynologist and can usually identify a tree by examining just one of its pollen grains. Palynologists have even been able to reconstruct ancient forest landscapes, long after all the leaves and wood of the trees have decayed, by examining the tough pollen grains that remained intact in sediments of lakes and ponds for thousands of years after they fell into the water.

Closely watch the insects that visit flowers. All of them are dusted with pollen during their visits, but only the bees actually collect pollen in special receptacles and store it for later use. Watch bees and notice how they comb the pollen from the hairs on their bodies with special brushes on their legs. Notice how even the eyes of honey bees are coated with long hairs. Honey bees transfer pollen to special "baskets" on their hind legs where the surface of the leg is scooped out and surrounded by

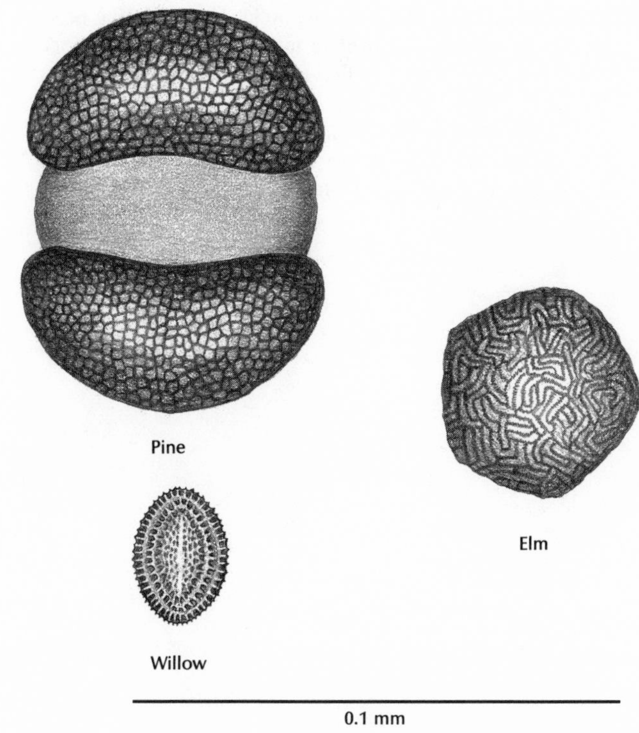


The distinctive pollen grains of three different trees.

long, curved hairs that hold the pollen. Leaf-cutting bees (p. 77) use an entirely different method for collecting pollen. They have special pollen-collecting hairs on the underside of their abdomens. All those hairs on a bee's body have important roles in pollen gathering.

Pollination triggers the development of seeds and fruits. Some seeds and fruits of trees form very soon after their flowers have been pollinated. Maples, elms, and willows are among those trees whose fruits ripen within weeks of pollination. The fruits and seeds of other trees like apples, oaks, and walnuts may take many months or even a couple of years to fully form. After you have discovered flowers on a tree, keep an eye on the fruits that subsequently start to form.

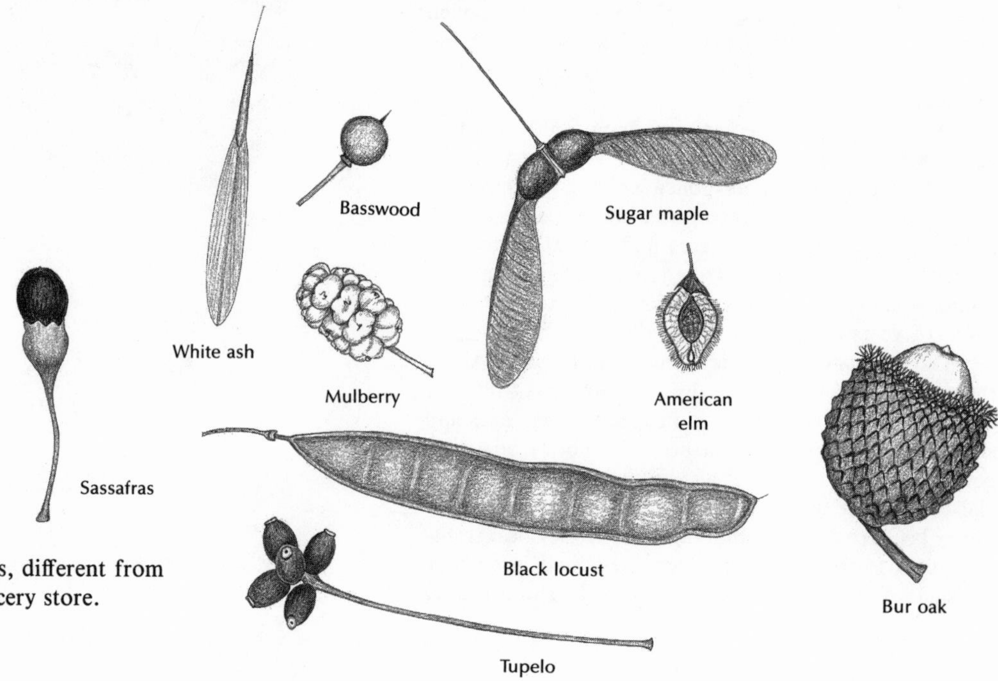


Fruits can be of many shapes, different from what we usually see in a grocery store.

# Trees and Galls

Where some animals fit into the vast web of interactions that links creatures with each other is often not as clear as the association of bees, flowers, and trees. When we consider all the creatures that live on a single tree and all the ways in which they can possibly be connected, it is surprising that we understand as much as we do.

In your own associations with trees, you may come across some structures called galls, which are neither buds nor fruits, flowers nor roots, twigs nor seeds. A gall is made entirely of tissue contributed by the tree as a cooperative effort between the tree and one or more insects or mites. Thousands of different galls are formed by thousands of different mites and insects. I cannot think of a single species of tree that does not have at least one type of gall. Most galls are found on oaks, and practically all of them are formed by the larvae of small and stingless gall wasps. Exactly how galls form is a mystery. The stimulus a gall maker provides that causes the tree to produce a gall must be very specific, since each gall is unique to a particular insect or mite. Besides being unique, some of these galls are very ornate and lovely.

The wool-sower gall is an amazingly complex structure formed on twigs of white oaks each spring. This gall looks like a ball of wool an inch in diameter and is home to several hundred tiny wasps, each of which develops in one of the several hundred pink chambers that are suspended within a web of gossamer strands. The chambers are evenly spaced throughout the gall and are joined by delicate strands that radiate from each chamber.

The mother of the wasps that emerge from the wool-sower gall laid her eggs on a bud of a white oak weeks earlier, perhaps while snow still covered the ground and certainly before new oak leaves had begun to appear. Since there were no male wasps for her to mate with, her sons and daughters were conceived without a father. Unlike their mother, these sons and daughters mate but produce only daughters.

As you are probably beginning to realize, gall wasps have some peculiar family histories. Each year there are two generations of wasps—a spring generation

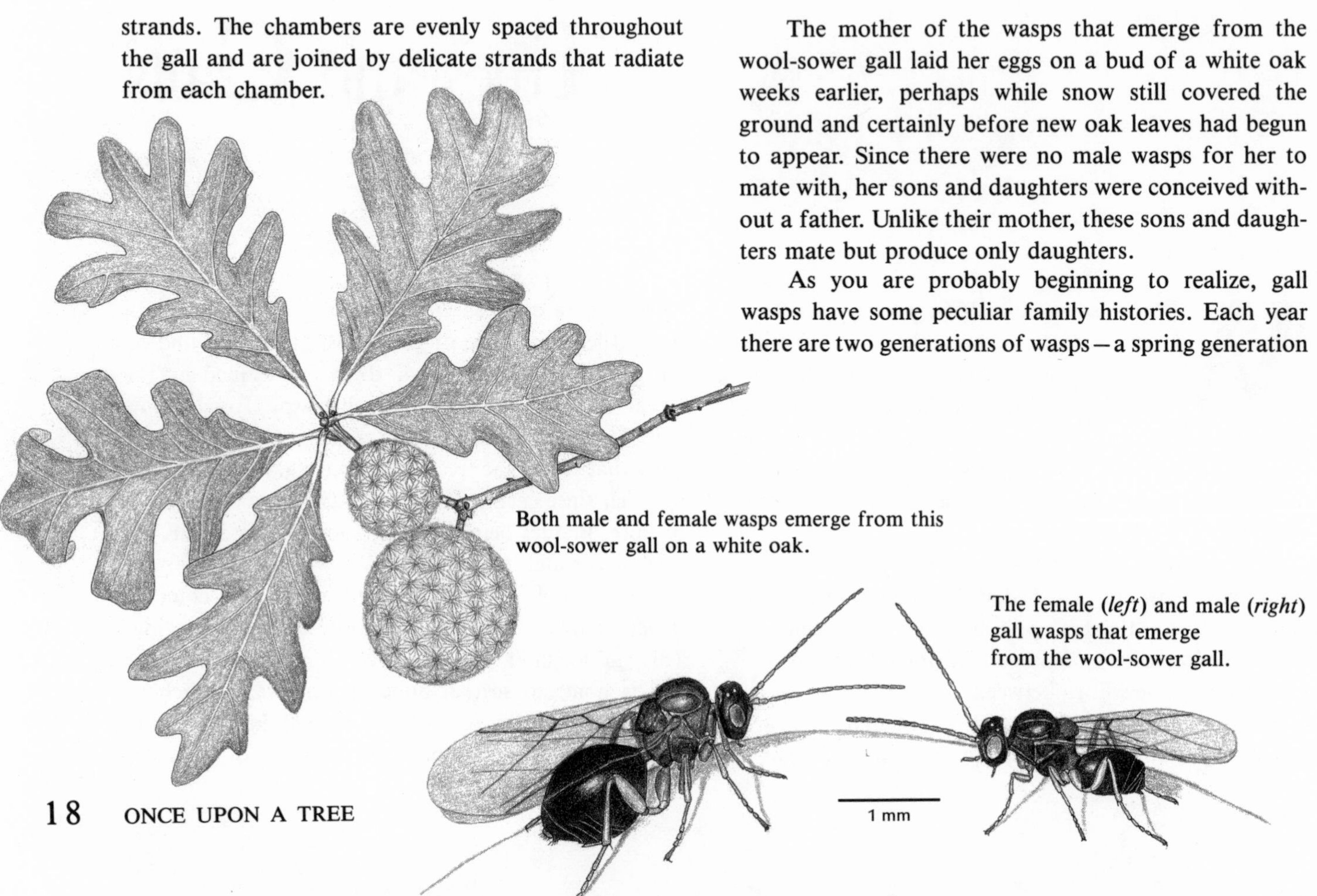


Both male and female wasps emerge from this wool-sower gall on a white oak.

The female (*left*) and male (*right*) gall wasps that emerge from the wool-sower gall.

and an overwintering generation—each forming its own unique gall. All members of the overwintering generation are females, but their offspring are both males and females produced without male parents. After these males and females mate, the cycle begins anew, and only daughters hatch from the eggs that they lay. The daughters look more like their grandmothers than they do their own parents. They also overwinter in galls like those of their grandmothers and not like those of their parents. A year in the life of a gall wasp family is often so complex that the complete family histories of most gall wasps are still unknown. No one knows, for example, where wasps from the wool-sower gall lay their eggs and in what galls their daughters and mothers live. The wasp of the oak hedgehog gall is one of the few gall wasps whose entire life cycle is known.

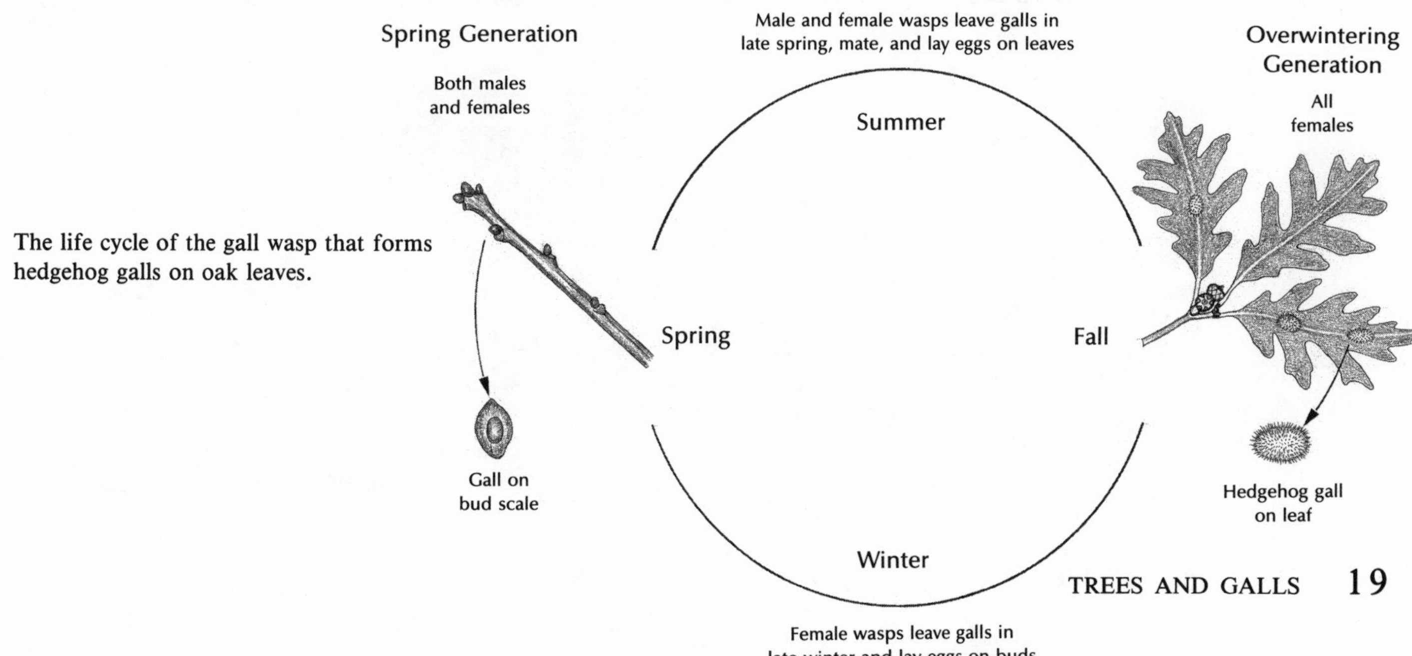


The life cycle of the gall wasp that forms hedgehog galls on oak leaves.

Because the two generations of wasps in each life cycle look different and live in different recognizable galls, many gall wasps have probably been described as separate species when they really are the same species. Learning how the lives of gall wasps are connected with the lives of oak trees is a job for a very careful and patient observer.

Gall wasps have few large predators except for woodpeckers that sometimes try to peck their way into the galls. The most worrisome enemies of gall insects are small parasitic wasps, such as the torymid wasps, that lay their eggs on the gall maker. The parasitic torymid wasp is about the same size as a gall wasp; but instead of being shiny black or brown like the gall wasp, the torymid wasp is a shiny, lustrous green. The female torymid has a sabrelike ovipositor that is longer than her body. During egg laying this ovipositor can reach even the innermost chambers of a gall. The many fine

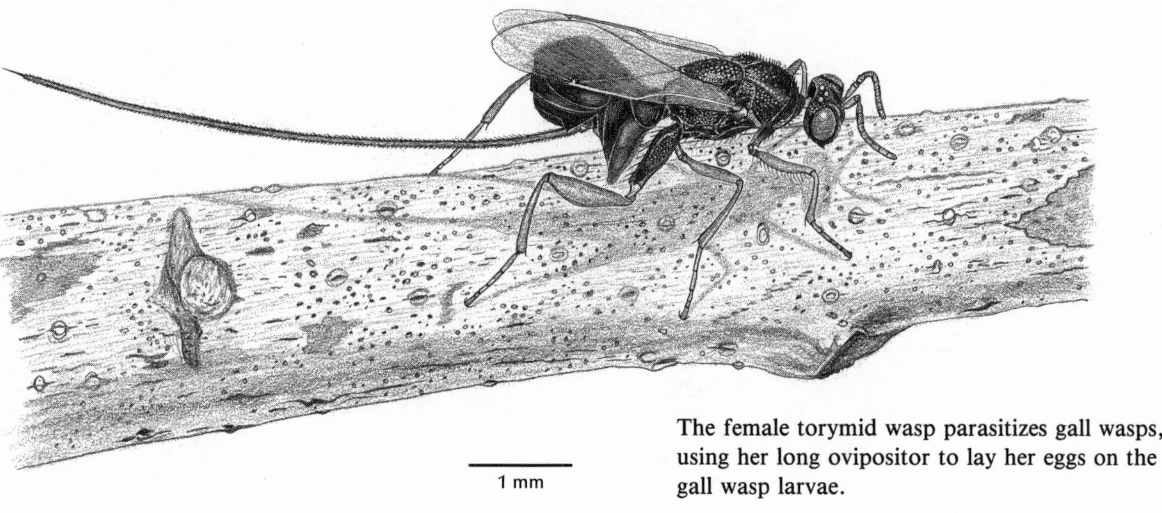


The female torymid wasp parasitizes gall wasps, using her long ovipositor to lay her eggs on the gall wasp larvae.

bristles that cover the ovipositor are sensitive to touch, and help guide the ovipositor toward the larvae that lie unseen inside the gall. The eggs of the parasitic wasp hatch into larvae that devour their hosts and take over the gall. What hatches from a gall can be either the gall maker or the parasitic wasp that devoured it or even another small wasp called an inquiline—a squatter that may move into the spacious, unoccupied quarters provided by the tissue of the gall.

The significance of gall wasps is just as much a mystery as the way in which their galls are formed. What good these wasps do to the tree, or for that matter to any creature of the tree, often may not be obvious to us. But how can anyone expect to appreciate all the ways in which creatures interact with one another? Because we still have so much to understand, the ways of nature often seem unclear and mysterious. In fairness to wasps and trees, however, we should appreciate galls for their own sake, if for no other reason.

## LEARNING FROM TREES

Galls can be collected from a tree or the ground beneath a tree at any season of the year. If galls are still attached to a green leaf or twig, cut the end of the twig or leaf and wrap it with a wet paper towel before placing it in a jar with a loose-fitting lid. You can also place the twig or the leaf in a vial of water with a cotton plug and then put the vial in the jar. As long as the twig or leaf is kept wet, the gall makers should continue developing inside their galls. Those galls collected in the fall or winter can be placed in a jar and left outdoors or in an unheated room. When warm weather finally arrives, the gall maker, a parasitic wasp, or an inquiline will sally forth into the daylight. You will find it flitting about in your jar.

A jar for rearing gall wasps.

Although oak trees have more types of galls than most trees, willows, elms, hackberries, and hickories also have some distinctively shaped galls. Willows have galls that resemble pine cones. Some galls on elm leaves look like cockscombs and some galls on hickory leaves look like small cones. Hackberry leaves are often covered with nipple galls (p. 34). Tiny mites are responsible for the small, knobby galls on leaves of maples, basswoods, and wild cherries (p. 58). See how many different shapes of galls you can find. Gently open a few of these galls and see if "anybody" is home, and if so, who it is.

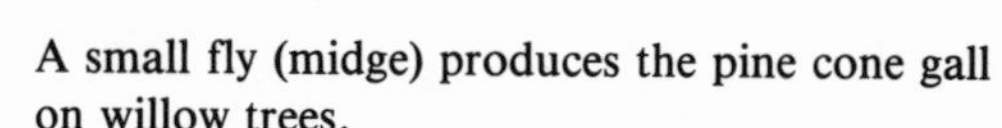

A small fly (midge) produces the pine cone gall on willow trees.

# Fungi, Roots, and Fungus Beetles

We are just beginning to understand some of the many unexpected events that occur in the soil under a tree. The dark world of the soil supports a rich variety of life forms that have established complex and mutually beneficial interactions with each other as well as with trees. What few glimpses we have had into this dark world reveal a web of relationships just as complex as those we encounter in the treetops.

In a bucket of soil from beneath a tree in the forest, a phenomenal number of life forms can be found—billions of bacteria, millions of single-celled animals called protozoa, thousands of fungi, mites, insects, and other tiny arthropods, as well as a few worms and snails. They all recycle dead plant and animal matter that has fallen to the ground and return a long list of soluble nutrients to the soil, water, and air. These nutrients can once again begin their journey through the tree through the tree community.

In addition to recycling nutrients for trees, some fungi of the soil have developed more intimate relationships with trees. The roots of certain trees intertwine with long strands of underground fungi, and these roots together with the fungi form what are called mycorrhizae. The trees and fungi both share and benefit from this special arrangement. The strands of fungi transfer water and minerals from the soil to the tree, and the tree shares its sugary sap with the fungi. Trees and fungi are dependent on each other for their well-being.

Fungi that develop mycorrhizae with the roots of

one tree can also join with the roots of other nearby trees, creating a complex web of interactions beneath the forest floor. Plant physiologists have shown that labeled chemicals can be transferred from one tree to another when the two are connected by underground fungi. Even in the shadows of towering trees, tiny seedlings that have joined the network of roots and fungi can grow and share in the abundance of nutrients that are constantly being exchanged underground.

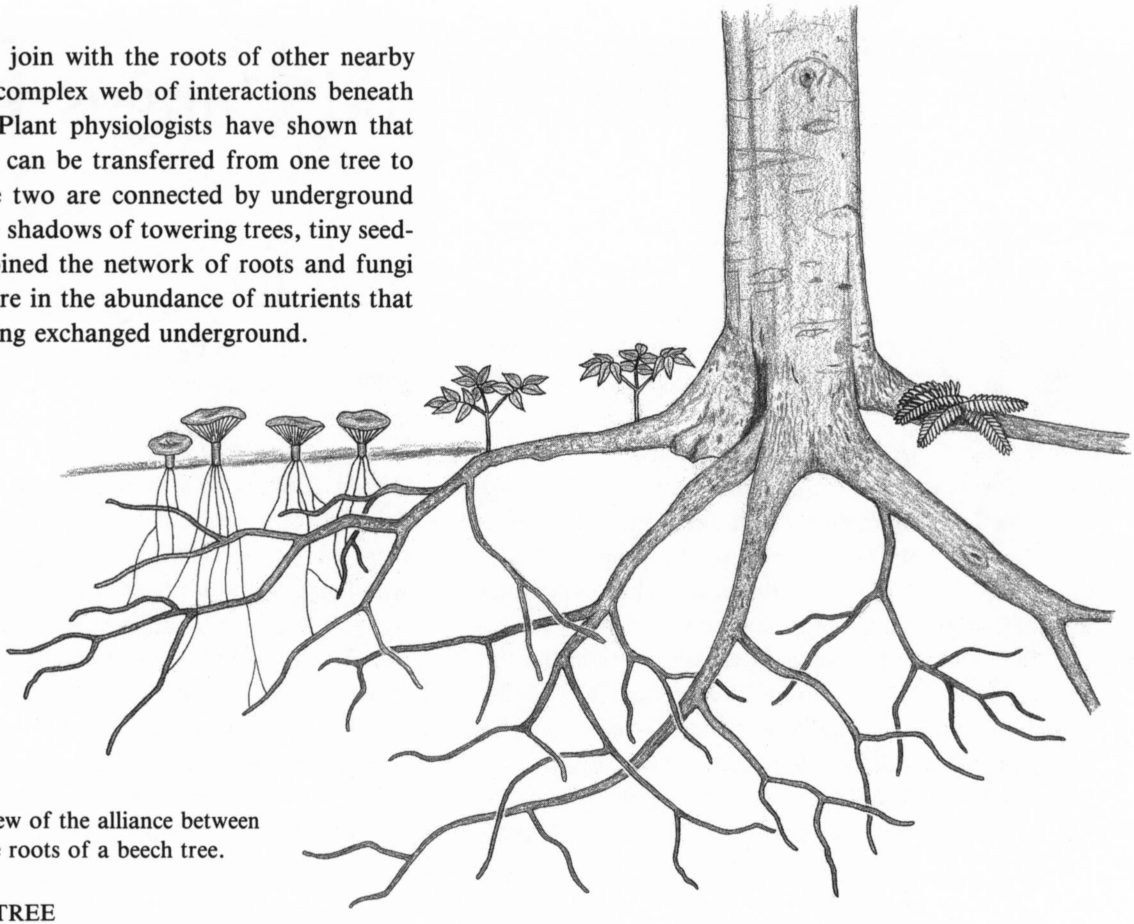

An underground view of the alliance between mushrooms and the roots of a beech tree.

At the end of summer, after the fungi have stored up enough of the sugars produced by the tree, they send strands from the roots to the surface of the soil and finally use the sugars in the production of mushrooms. And what a colorful display it can be! Red, orange, blue, green, yellow, and brown mushrooms can carpet the forest floor on a day in late summer or autumn. The mushrooms that pop up under trees after a rainy spell are formed by thousands of intertwined strands of fungi. Before the rain, the strands of fungi were scattered among the soil and roots, actively decomposing fallen branches and leaves. In some amazing and mysterious way, individual strands of fungi come together, grow, and form the unique shapes of mushrooms aboveground. From these mushrooms come the spores that are carried off by the wind or fungus beetles to start new fungi and mushrooms elsewhere.

2 mm

The fungus beetle spreads mushroom spores along its trails.

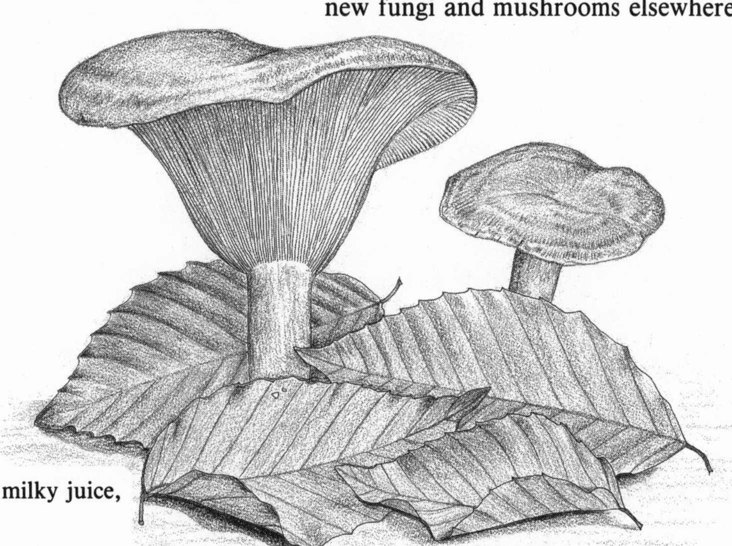

Milk mushrooms, named for their milky juice, and beech leaves.

Fungus beetles live on mushrooms, they feed on mushrooms, and they undoubtedly spread the spores of mushrooms. During the day the beetles rest and at night they set out on their travels from tree to tree and from mushroom to mushroom. Many of the spores they leave along their trails will sprout and form new mycorrhizae. Trees, fungi, and beetles all seem to benefit from this alliance.

In the forests of the Pacific Northwest, other fungi, called truffles, form mycorrhizal partnerships with the roots of spruce and hemlock trees. Unlike mushrooms, truffles live and set spores entirely underground where neither wind nor most fungus beetles can reach them. But in the spruce and hemlock forests, flying squirrels have taken over the job of spreading the truffle spores. The noses of flying squirrels are "tuned into" the pungent scent of the truffles that lie beneath the forest floor. They dig up the buried fungi and eagerly devour them, scattering the spores in their droppings.

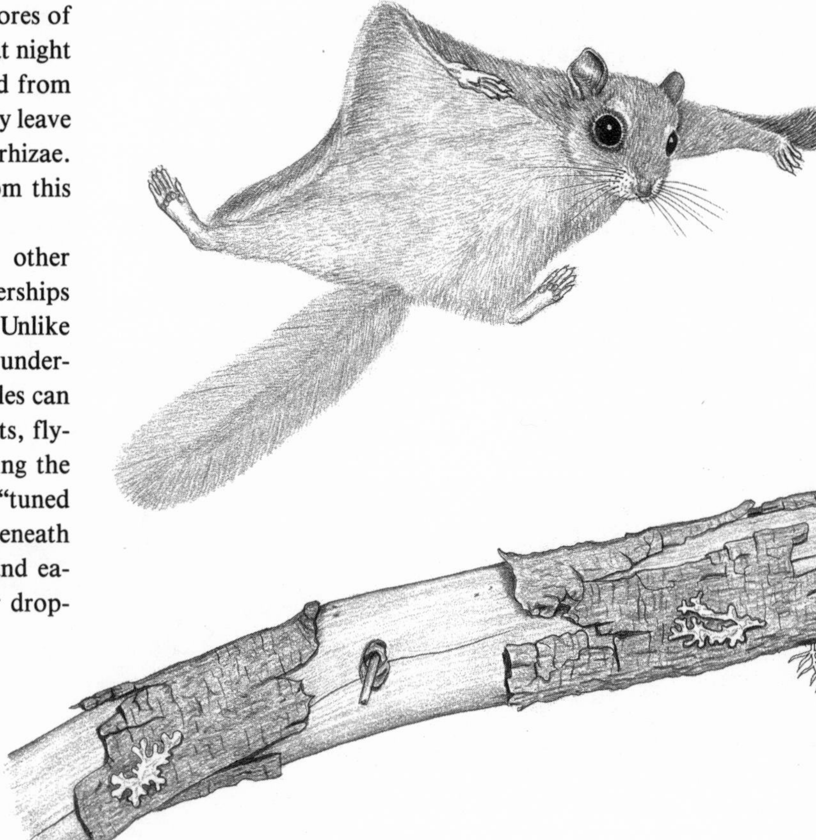

Flying squirrels spread the truffle spores in spruce and hemlock forests.

## LEARNING FROM TREES

If you dig into the bed of fallen leaves beneath a tree, you will often see white, yellow, or orange strands of fungi covering the surfaces of decaying leaves and branches. These fungal strands are breaking down the dead plant and animal matter that lies scattered beneath the tree. As the fungi go about the business of decomposing the leaf litter, they recycle nutrients that have been and will be used again and again by the tree and its companions.

Notice how certain mushrooms are found under certain trees. Because trees and fungi are selective in establishing their mycorrhizal partnerships, an experienced mushroom hunter will know under which trees certain mushrooms are most likely to be found. The next time you find mushrooms, see what other animals are also checking them out. Mushroom hunting has many rewards, including some for the taste buds. Remember, however, that some mushrooms are very beautiful but **very** poisonous. **NEVER** taste or eat any mushroom unless you know exactly what it is and whether it is edible.

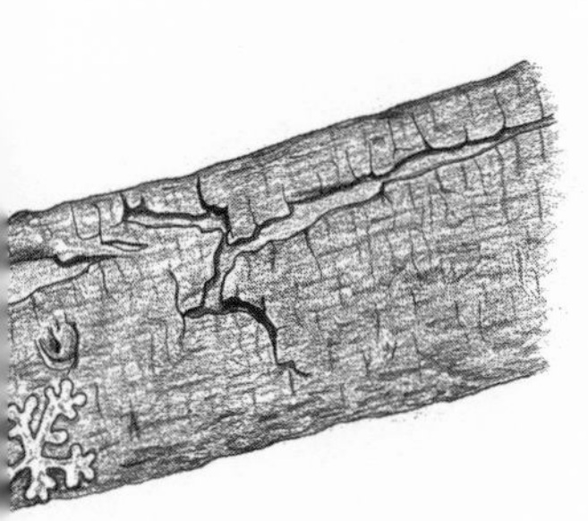

Morels are very tasty, edible mushrooms often found under elm and apple trees as well as under oak and ash trees.

If you look on the underside of a mushroom cap, you will see the many gills that produce thousands of spores. Some of these spores are carried by fungus beetles and flies that visit mushrooms. Other spores are dispersed in the droppings of small mammals. You can prepare a spore print of a mushroom cap and learn how many spores a single mushroom can produce and what the spores look like. Remove the cap of a mushroom from its stem and place it, gills down, on a sheet of paper. Use light-colored paper for mushrooms with dark spores and dark-colored paper for mushrooms with light spores. Leave the cap undisturbed by covering it with a bowl or jar for several hours or overnight. When you gently lift the mushroom cap from the paper and examine the print, you will see how the spores are arranged in that particular mushroom. Different mushrooms have spores of different colors as well as different arrangements. Examine the spores with a magnifier or microscope and observe their shapes, colors, and sizes. By carefully spraying the spore print with lacquer or a charcoal fixative, you can preserve the print. See how many different kinds of mushrooms you can find so you can discover just how different their spores are.

Thousands of spores, just one of which can form a mycorrhizal partnership with tree roots, make up these spore prints of a mushroom.

# Sap and Sapsuckers

Sap flows from treetop to root tip. In the roots, the sap picks up minerals and water. In the leaves, it picks up the sugars that are produced by photosynthesis when carbon dioxide from the air is combined with water from the soil. After various parts of the tree have taken their share of nutrients from the sap, there are still enough left over for the birds and the insects known as sapsuckers.

A single sugar maple, apple tree, or tulip tree may have several thousand tiny holes arranged in neat rows around its trunk and branches. This is the unmistakable work of a woodpecker called the yellow-bellied sapsucker. This bird can spend hours tapping out neat rows of holes on the trunks of trees that have particularly sugary sap. The sap that the sapsuckers are so fond of

A yellow-bellied sapsucker searches for a sugary snack on a tulip tree.

oozes out of these holes. Insects soon discover the oozing sap, and the birds are quick to snatch up some of these crunchy insects along with the sweet sap.

The sap from tree roots is just as nourishing and tasty as the sap from the branches, twigs, and leaves. Certain insects spend most of their lives feeding exclusively on this root sap. For many long years, the nymphs of periodical cicadas inhabit the dark world of tree roots. Three species of these cicadas spend 13 years underground, and three other species spend 17 years among the roots. Here they feed and grow on the sap that flows through even the tiniest roots. The spring eventually arrives when it is time for each nymph to dig its way to the surface, shed its skin, and spread its wings that have been forming during all those years spent underground. As the cicadas emerge from the soil, the ground beneath the trees on which they have been feeding may be pitted with thousands of holes, each about a half inch across. The time has finally come for the nymph to complete metamorphosis to the adult stage.

The colorful adult cicadas, with red eyes and orange wings, now cover trees in vast numbers as they go about their courting. Males emerge from their nymphal shells shortly before the females and quickly gather in

After 17 years underground, the periodical cicada crawls onto a branch to shed its nymphal skin (*bottom*) and spread its colorful wings (*top*).

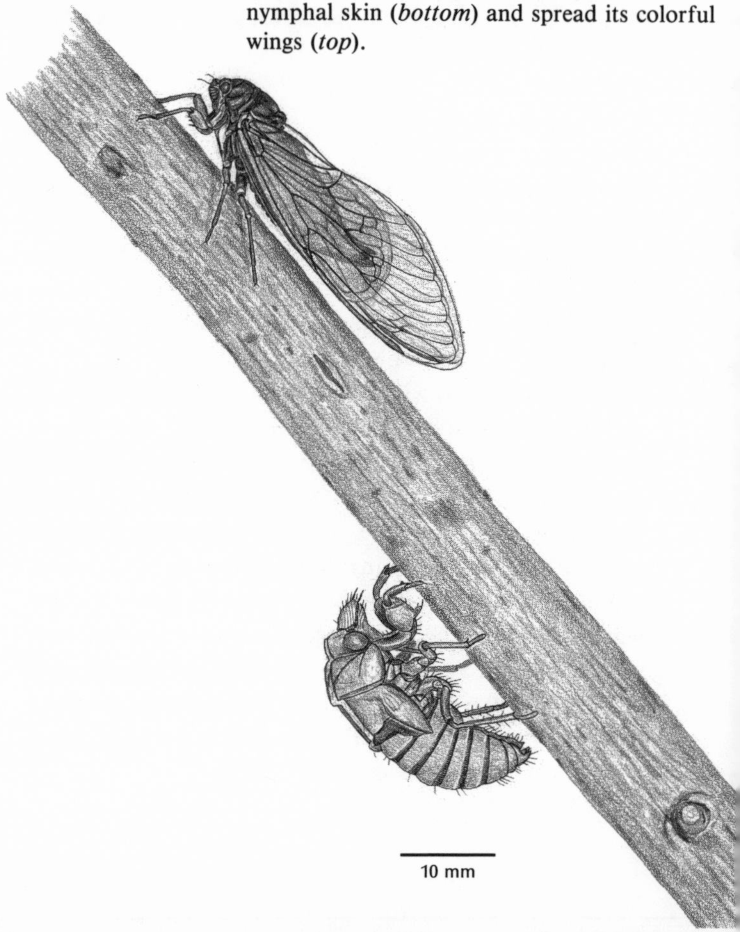

10 mm

groups, each consisting of as many as several thousand individuals. Each group of males is called a "chorus center" because once the males have gathered together they begin producing the loud whining **"burr-r-r"** for which they are so well known. Male cicadas do not have vocal cords to produce their long and loud songs. Instead, they rapidly vibrate a pair of stretched membranes called drums that are found in an inner chamber of the body. The sound produced in a chorus center can be deafening, but the loud **"burr-r-r"** is evidently appealing to female cicadas. The females flock to the chorus centers to mate and then lay their eggs on twigs and branches.

Within a matter of days, the thousands of noisy cicadas disappear from the trees, and tiny cicada nymphs hatch from the eggs. As soon as they fall to the ground, they begin their long, hidden journeys through the soil for 17, or at least 13, more years. The sight and sounds of the hordes of cicadas that cover the trees for a brief time, however, are not readily forgotten.

Nymphs of other cicadas share root sap with nymphs of periodical cicadas, but these other cicada nymphs spend at least 4 but fewer than 13 years underground. These shorter-lived cicadas are often larger than the periodical cicadas, but they emerge from the soil in far fewer numbers. And their eyes and wings are not nearly as colorful as those of the periodical cicadas.

While cicada nymphs are at work below ground, other related insects are tapping sap in the treetops. Among the many other species of sap-sucking insects, lace bugs are probably the most elegant looking; but, being only about one-eighth inch long, they usually go unnoticed and unappreciated. Although tiny, they are abundant. A single sycamore tree can have more than a million lace bugs scattered over the lower surfaces of its leaves.

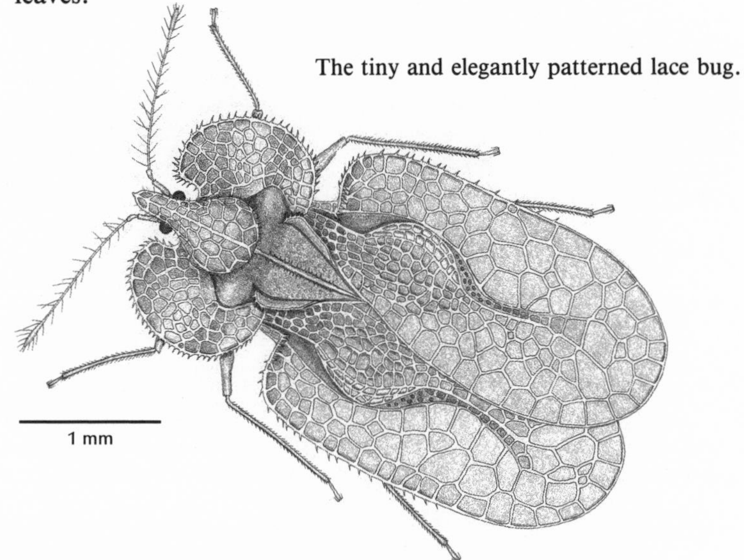


The tiny and elegantly patterned lace bug.

Some even smaller insects called aphids can be found on either leaves or roots, in the company of lace bugs as well as cicadas. For most of the spring and summer, only female aphids are found on trees, and they constantly give birth to live young that are also all females. When the leaf or root on which they are feeding becomes too crowded, the aphids begin to grow wings and fly off to new feeding grounds. Only at the end of summer do male aphids make a brief appearance, to fertilize the eggs that will overwinter on the tree.

Ants have a special fondness for sweet things and often travel far from their underground nests to harvest the sap that passes completely through aphids and appears as droppings of sweet, clear liquid called honeydew. Some simply stay underground and adopt root-feeding aphids as nest mates and a source for honeydew. Ants may collect aphid eggs in the autumn and carry them to their nest. Here the eggs are tended during the winter until the newly hatched aphids wander off to feed on tiny roots. In the spring, ants sometimes carry overwintering eggs of aphids from the base

An adult ant will shepherd aphids and, in return, get some of the honeydew secreted by the aphids.

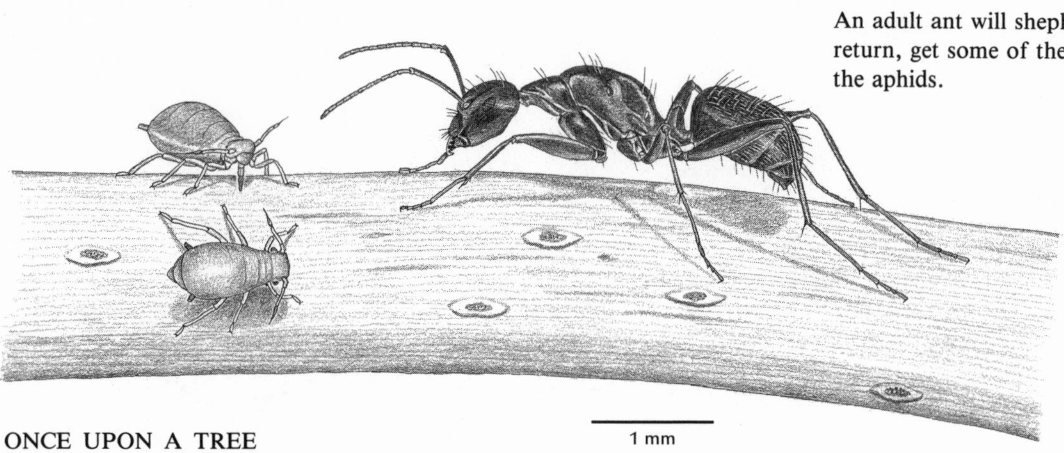

of a tree to the upper branches as new leaves unfold. In return for the secondhand sap that they receive from the aphids, ants protect them from their predators and will challenge ladybird beetles, ladybird larvae, or aphid lions that try to eat "their" aphids.

Aphid lions are the larvae of lacewings (p. 93) and are particularly formidable-looking predators of aphids. With their hollow, sickle-shaped jaws, these larvae impale aphids and then, in vampire fashion, drain them of their blood.

Among the strangest, if not the strangest, sapsuckers are the scale insects. These peculiar creatures spend most of their lives on twigs, hidden beneath shells constructed from a mixture of their shed skins and waxy secretions from special glands. Late in the summer males crawl out from beneath their shells. They have wings, eyes, and legs, but no mouthparts. Their days of feeding are over, and they are fated to die after mating. Females do have mouthparts, but they lack eyes, wings, and legs and never leave their shells, not even for mating or egg laying. The shell of the dead mother protects her eggs during the weeks of winter. In the spring, the

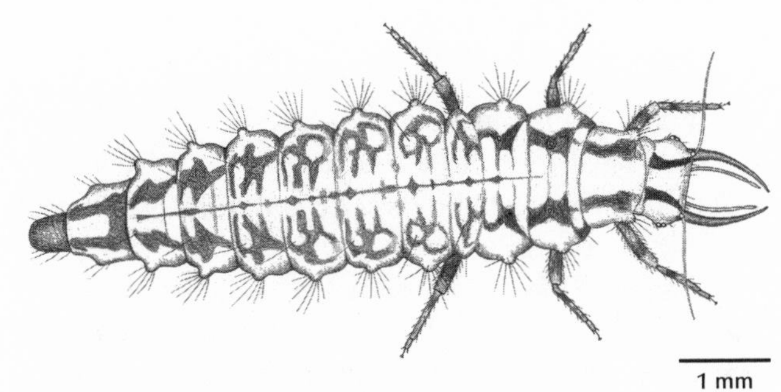

The fierce-looking aphid lion, or lacewing larva.

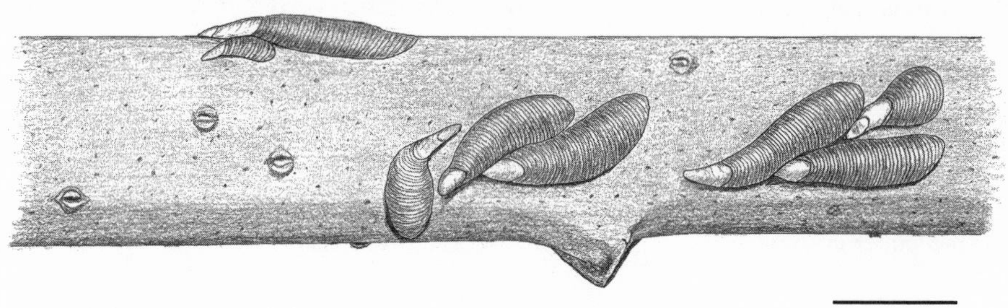

Oyster scales on an apple twig.

newly hatched nymphs or "crawlers" set off from their mother's shell to claim a new area of twig. Here each will settle down to build its scale and drill for sap until the end of summer.

Some of the other insects that suck sap with their sharp beaks may be unknown and inconspicuous because they are as tiny as the aphids, lace bugs, and scale insects. Others may be unknown to us because they look so much like the twig, leaf, or bark on which they are found that we don't recognize them. Their disguises may save them from hungry birds that happen to be around.

## LEARNING FROM TREES

Aphids and some relatives of aphids, called psyllids, are sometimes found in galls on leaves. And like these aphids, psyllid nymphs are sapsuckers. Inside their galls where they suck the sap of leaves, aphids and young psyllids are sheltered from the sun and rain as well as from many predators. Two galls that can be extremely plentiful and easily spotted are the hackberry nipple galls of psyllids and the cottonwood petiole galls of aphids. Only in late summer or early autumn do adult aphids and adult psyllids leave their galls to spend the winter in some sheltered spot. The adult psyllids that fly from hackberry galls look remarkably like tiny cicadas that are about 2–3 millimeters long.

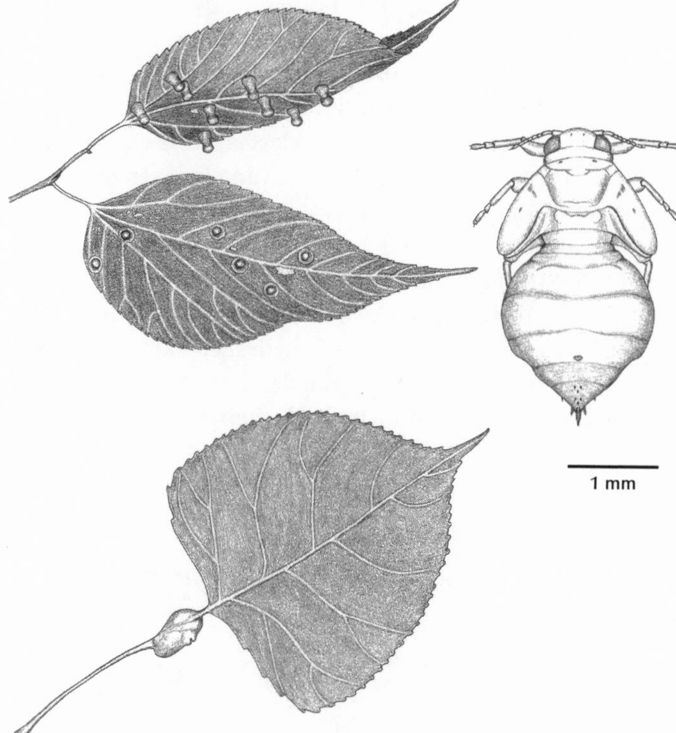


A psyllid nymph, with developing wings, lives inside a nipple gall on a hackberry leaf (*top*). A cottonwood leaf with a petiole gall from which aphids will eventually emerge (*bottom*).

One obvious feature that sapsuckers have in common, whether they are birds or insects, is that they all use beaks to poke around for tree sap. The sharp beaks neatly pierce the outer layers of bark, twigs, or leaves to reach the sap flowing beneath the surface. But insect beaks are not like bird beaks. Insect beaks are hollow, and they act like straws to draw up sap from the tree. Other insects, like caterpillars, beetles, crickets, and wasps, have jaws rather than beaks that they use for chewing. If you flip over a cicada, stink bug, or other sapsucker, you will see its long beak lying against its underside. Watch one of these insects as it sucks sap from a tree, and you will see its beak extending from beneath its head into the tissues of the tree.

As you watch, you may also notice that some sap taken up by an insect's beak reappears at the other end of the insect as droppings of honeydew. If there are enough sap-sucking insects on a tree (and there often are millions on a single tree), the leaves of the tree and the ground beneath the tree will be splattered with their sweet, sticky honeydew. Sometimes you can feel the fine droplets of honeydew that fall on your neck and arms as you walk beneath the tree. Some molds grow very well on the sugars and amino acids that make up honeydew. Many chewing insects, such as buprestid beetles, wasps, and some ants, graze on these patches of mold and honeydew. Probably as many different creatures feed on honeydew as feed on tree sap itself.

Note the long, hollow beak on the underside of a stink bug.

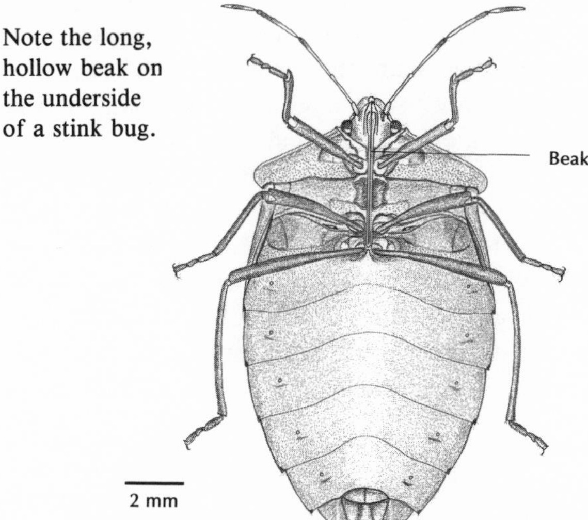


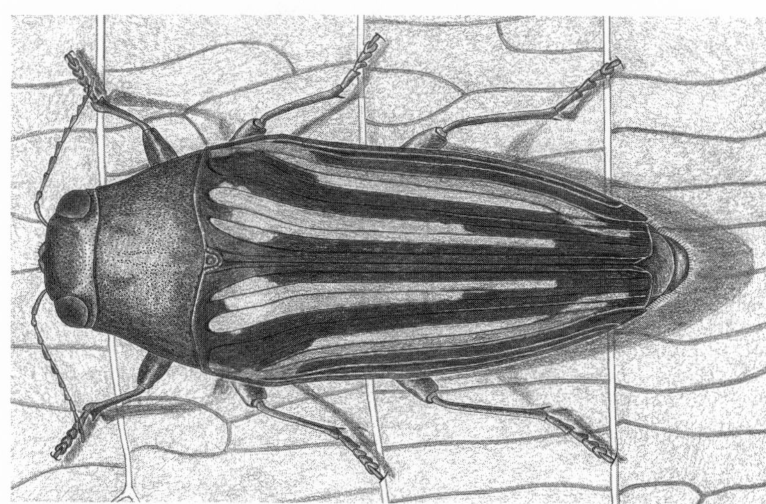


A buprestid beetle feeding on honeydew that coats a walnut leaf.

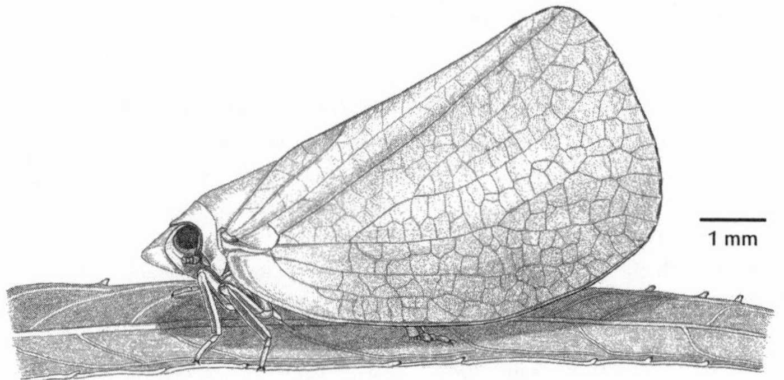


# Artful Deceptors

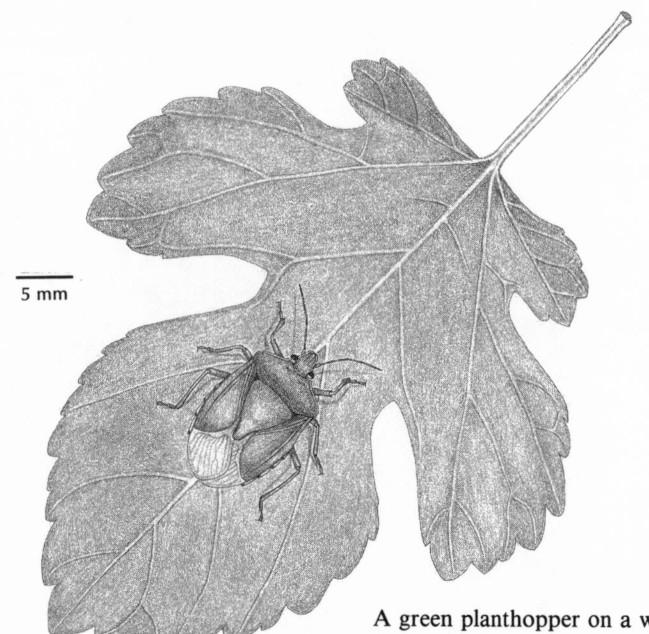


Deception is the chief defense that many animals use in dealing with predators. Animals can masquerade as any part of a tree, including lichens on bark and bird droppings on leaves. Their disguises are surprisingly good.

Green is a popular color for insects that live among green leaves. Green stink bugs and green planthoppers blend well with green leaves and green twigs. They can sit motionlessly sucking sap without anyone ever noticing them.

Another group of stink bugs are brown and gray and look like bits of bark. They roam trees in search of caterpillars and other insects. These stink bugs use their beaks to first stab their victims, then to inject them with digestive juices, and finally to suck out the body fluids



A green planthopper on a willow leaf (*top*). A green stink bug on a mulberry leaf (*bottom*).

of their prey. If these stink bugs are as inconspicuous to the eyes of other insects as they are to ours, they are probably very successful at ambushing their unsuspecting victims.

There are also treehoppers that, once they settle down and sink their beaks into a tree, look like just another spine or bump on the tree. They often look outlandish, covered with spines and knobs, from the moment they hatch from their eggs and begin sucking sap. However, the spines and knobs on young treehoppers sometimes look very little like those of their parents. The nymph of the buffalo treehopper loses a row of spines on its back for two horns on its head when it transforms into an adult. It is amazing what metamorphosis can do.

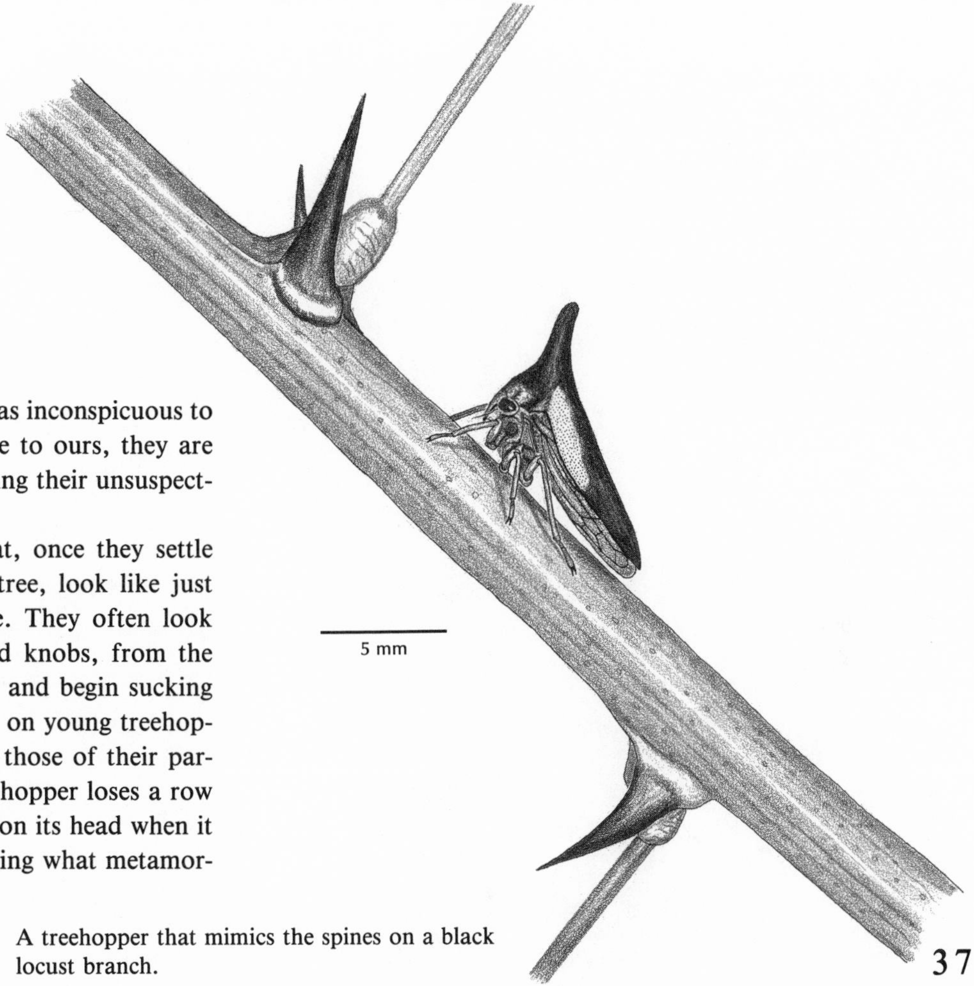

5 mm

A treehopper that mimics the spines on a black locust branch.

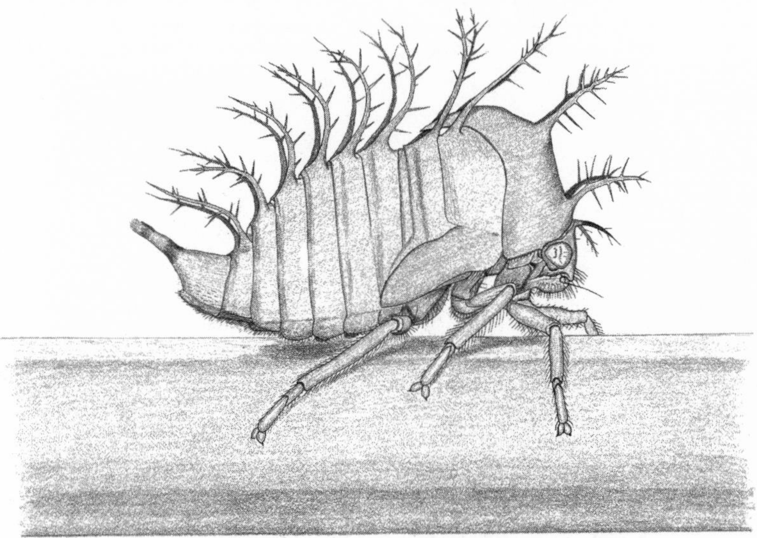


The buffalo treehopper nymph (*top*) will metamorphose into the adult buffalo treehopper (*bottom*).

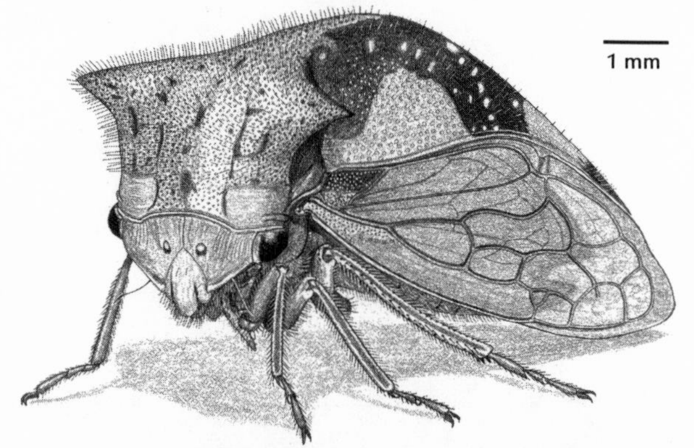


Walkingsticks and inchworms disguise themselves very successfully as twigs—sometimes green ones, sometimes brown ones—by posing motionlessly for long stretches of time. In between poses, walkingsticks move on to find new leaves to chew. Inchworms relax

The walkingstick is well named and is often hard to find unless you see it walking.

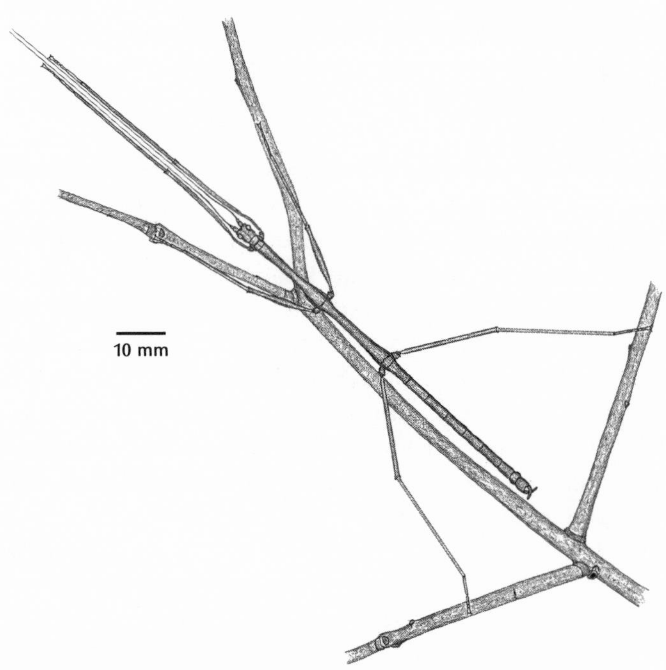

after their stiff poses and then slink off as only inchworms can. The inchworm begins to slink by first drawing its tail end up to its front end and forming a loop of all its body segments in between. It then extends its whole length forward. Once again the tail end catches up with the head end as the caterpillar methodically "inches" along a leaf or a twig.

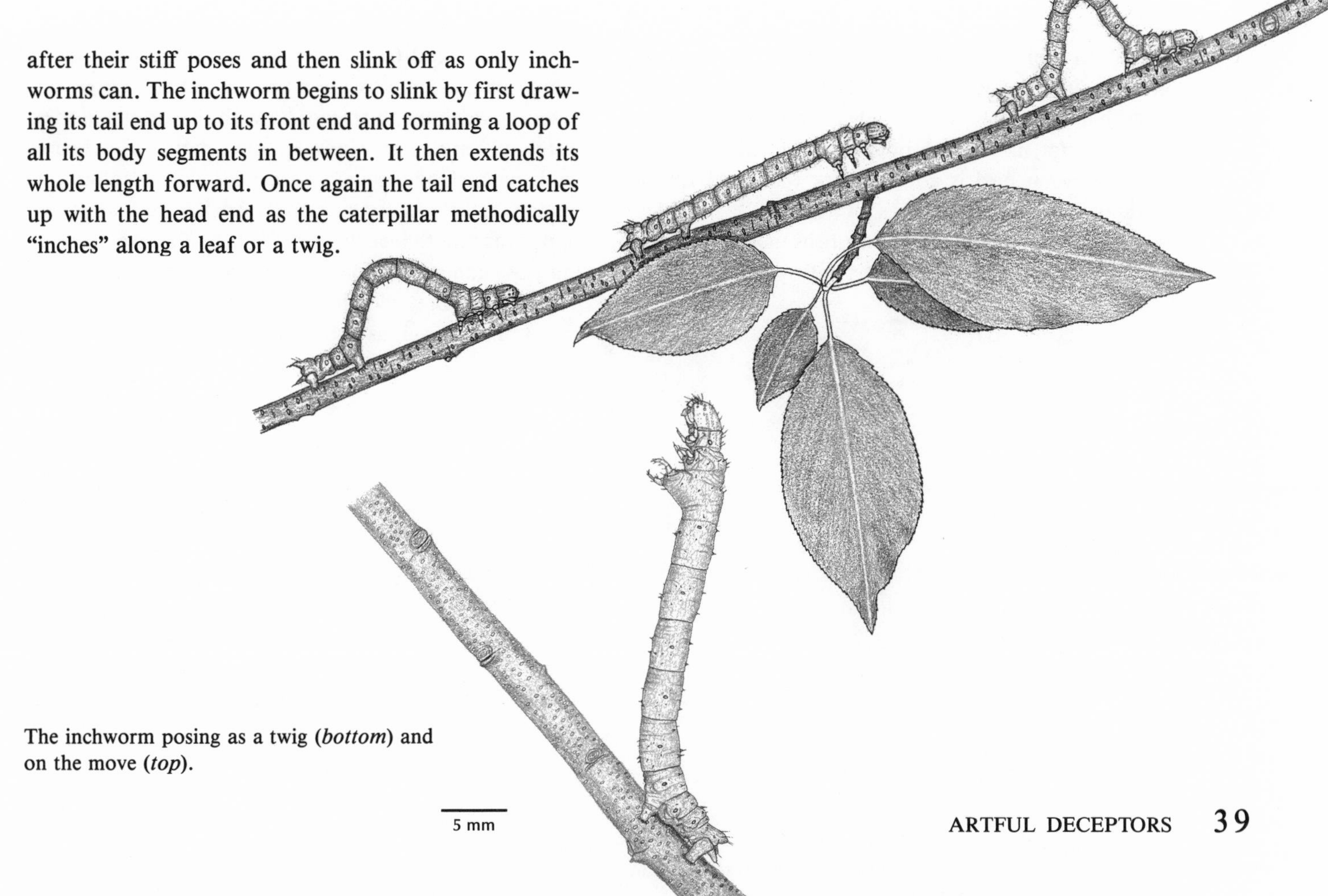


The inchworm posing as a twig (*bottom*) and on the move (*top*).

When a black and white tineid moth settles down on a leaf, it suddenly looks just like bird droppings. The birds that so eagerly devour other crawling and flying insects do not show much interest in these little moths. After all, what bird is going to risk the possibility of mistaking one of its droppings for a moth? By masquerading as something inedible, the tineid moth has found a way to live in peace with insect-eating birds.

Moths tend to spend a lot of time on tree bark. Many of these moths are attired in blacks, grays, and whites, which blend splendidly with the colors and textures of bark. The wings of some moths are covered with patches of greens, grays, and whites, colors that match the lichens growing on the bark of so many trees. Still other moths, such as noctuid moths, wear an all-purpose camouflage pattern of black, gray, green, yellow, and white splotches so they blend in with both plain bark as well as lichen-covered bark.

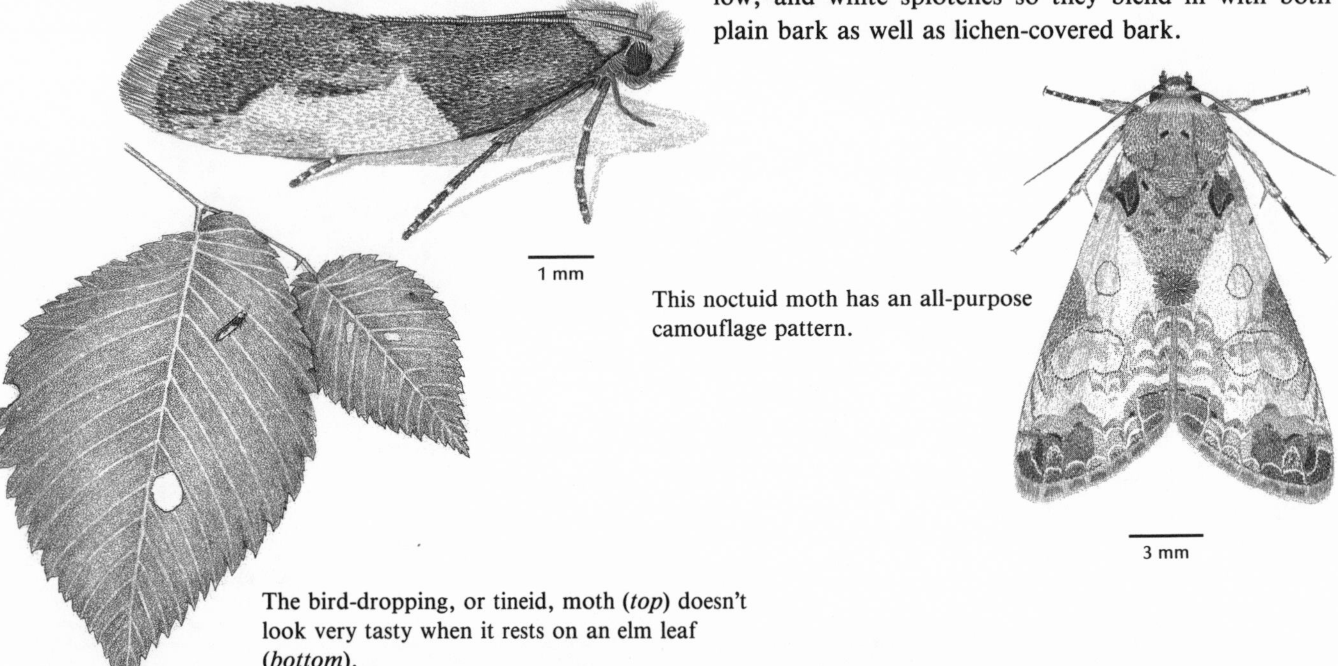


This noctuid moth has an all-purpose camouflage pattern.

The bird-dropping, or tineid, moth (*top*) doesn't look very tasty when it rests on an elm leaf (*bottom*).

An underwing moth's colorful hindwings (*above*) distract intruders. A startled possum in a basswood tree eyes an underwing moth that got away (*right*).

There are even some moths that use bright colors to aid them in their escapes. A bird or mammal that ventures too close to an underwing moth is in for a startling experience. The resting moth folds it forewings over its colorful hindwings (or underwings) and lies unnoticed against the bark of a tree. But if the moth is disturbed it flies off, flashing the bright colors of its underwings and startling the intruder long enough to assure escape.

The yellow, green, and gray lichens on tree bark are tiny plants that are part fungi and part algae. These unusual plants represent an extreme form of interdependence between two organisms. The algal member of the lichen partnership can live independently and often is found on its own; however, the fungal member is totally dependent on its algal partner for survival. The algal partner uses photosynthesis to manufacture sugars for the lichen, and the fungal partner extends tiny rootlike strands into the dead outer bark of trees. Over months and years, a lichen slowly decomposes the dead bark of the tree and uses whatever nutrients the bark can provide. These fragile-looking plants can readily endure the extremes of heat and cold to which they are exposed on bark, but they quickly disappear in the presence of just traces of air pollution.

As we zoom in with a magnifier or microscope for a closer look at lichens, we see that they form a forest of their own on branches and trunks of most trees. Certain caterpillars in one family of moths, the Arctiidae, live in this forest. They feed on lichens and live in cases that they construct from lichen fragments. Beetles, mites, and bark lice also move in the shadows of lichens. Vireos, hummingbirds, gnatcatchers, and pe-

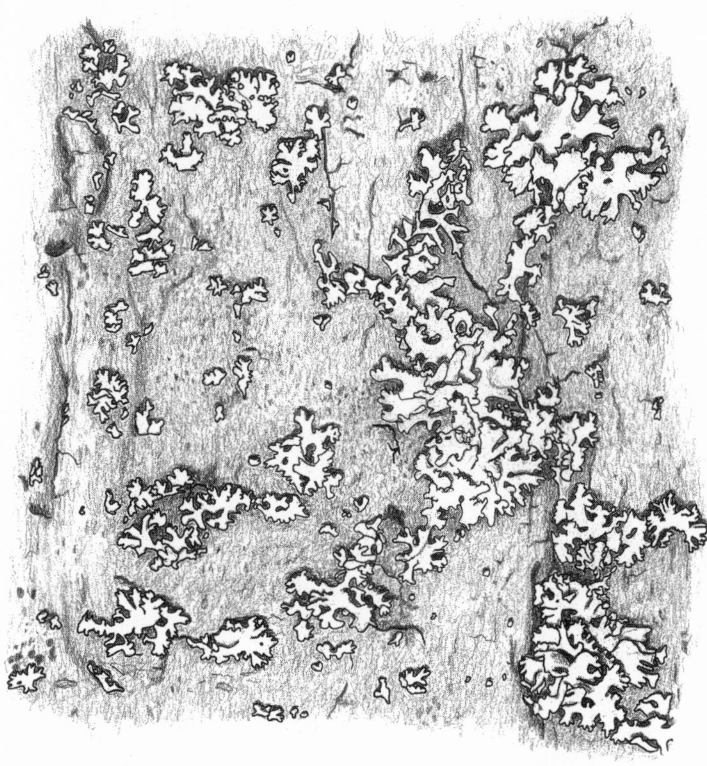

Lichens on sycamore bark.

wees often adorn their little nests with lichens that they collect from tree bark. With a coating of lichens, each nest looks like just another knob on a branch. Other birds like the brown creeper and nuthatch poke their beaks into lichen forests, for they have learned that every now and then they pull out a tasty insect.

A hummingbird and its tiny lichen-covered nest on a hemlock branch.

While birds pose a threat to insects during the day, tree frogs hunt for insects during the night. Like the insects they hunt, tree frogs do a little masquerading themselves to avoid the keen eyesight of even larger hunters—owls, raccoons, and possums. The skin of a tree frog is filled with pigment cells of different colors and shapes, and as the colors and textures of a frog's surroundings change, the color of the frog's skin changes to match its surroundings.

The interplay of light with various pigment cells is responsible for the changes in skin color of the tree frog. Sunlight is made up of many colors—red, orange, yellow, green, blue, indigo, violet. All these colors of sunlight pass through the outermost epidermal cells of the frog's skin and interact with the different pigment cells—lipophores, guanophores, and melanophores—deeper in the skin. Some colors of light are absorbed by the cells, and some colors are reflected toward our eyes. The only colors that we actually see are the colors that are reflected by the pigment cells. As sunlight passes through the skin of a green tree frog, lipophores first absorb the blue and violet colors. Next, the guanophores reflect the green light. Each guanophore is surrounded by a melanophore. The black pigment granules

A tree frog sitting on a sycamore leaf.

of the melanophore can absorb all colors of light and can move around within each cell. In green tree frogs, the black pigment lies at the base of (beneath) each guanophore and absorbs whatever colors remain after light first interacts with guanophores. Only the green light reflected by the guanophores remains unabsorbed and reaches our eyes. In gray or brown tree frogs, black pigment has spread throughout each melanophore and actually engulfs guanophore cells. Sunlight that passes through the skin of a dark tree frog is never reflected from guanophore cells since the black pigment covering each guanophore absorbs practically all colors of light before any colors can be reflected to our eyes. What our eyes see is a dark image. As the black pigment granules shift within the melanophores, the skin of a tree frog can take on any shade of color between the greens of leaves to the grays and browns of bark.

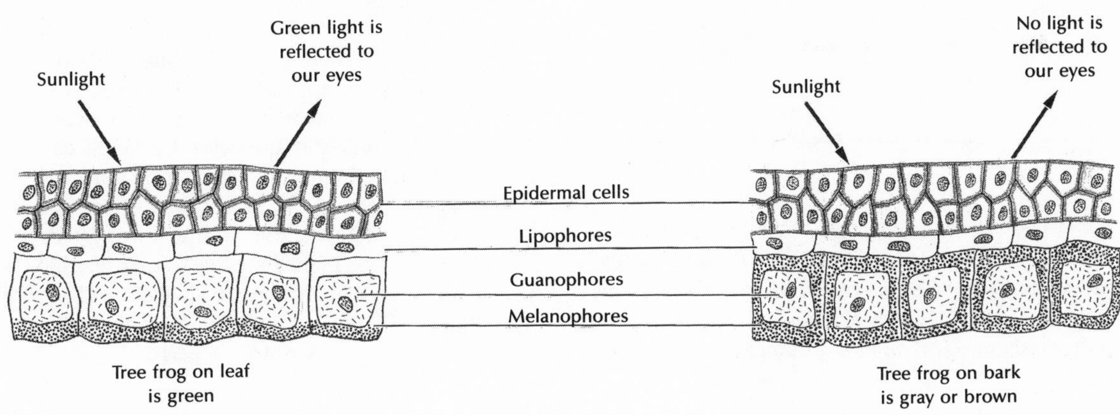


Cross sections of tree frog skin showing how sunlight interacts with the pigment cells when the frog appears green on a green leaf (*left*) and when the frog appears dark on the bark of the tree (*right*).

The artful deceptors of a tree certainly do not draw attention to themselves, and they sometimes need a little coaxing to reveal their whereabouts. Try placing a white sheet under a branch of a tree and then rap the branch with a large stick. After a sharp jolt to the branch, many insects, spiders, and mites will probably fall to the sheet. You will most likely dislodge a number of creatures that you did not expect to see.

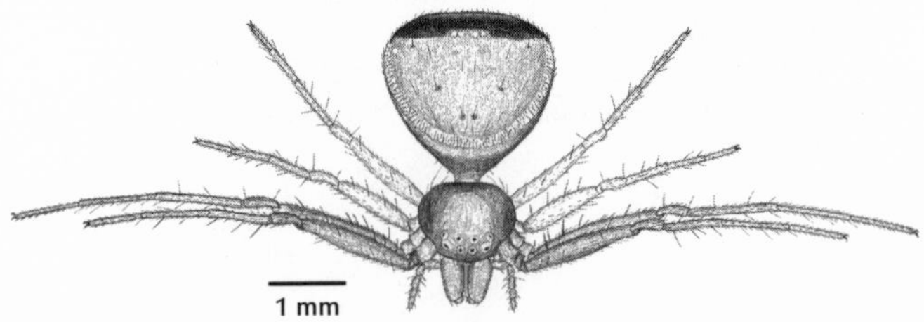


A crab spider ready to ambush insects.

Every tree has its caterpillars—fuzzy, spiny, bumpy, and smooth—for wherever there are moths and butterflies, there must also be caterpillars. Inchworms may dangle from leaves by silken threads. Some caterpillars may pose as edges of leaves, bird droppings, or twigs; but the bright colors of other caterpillars stand out conspicuously against the green of the leaves.

A caterpillar seems to be just as content in a large glass jar as on the tree where it was found. As long as a caterpillar always has a fresh supply of leaves from that tree, it will steadily chew away until it can grow no more. When that happens, the time has come for its metamorphosis. The caterpillar of a butterfly forms a chrysalis when it transforms from larva to pupa. Some caterpillars of moths spin cocoons and pupate on the leaves where they have fed for days and weeks; others wander far from their leafy homes and burrow into the ground to pupate without spinning a cocoon. In case one of these wandering caterpillars is living in your glass jar, it is probably a good idea to put an inch or two of moist soil in the bottom of the jar.

The pupal stage may last a few days or as long as several months. If a moth or butterfly does not appear after a month, it is not likely to appear until the coming spring. During the winter months many cocoons are easy to spot on branches and twigs. Leave the cocoon, chrysalis, or naked pupa outside during the cold months of winter. When the first warm days of spring arrive, bring the jar inside again and wait a few more days or weeks while the insect completes its transformation. Be sure to place an upright stick in the jar. The newly emerged moth or butterfly will need to climb up this stick in order to spread and dry its wings properly.

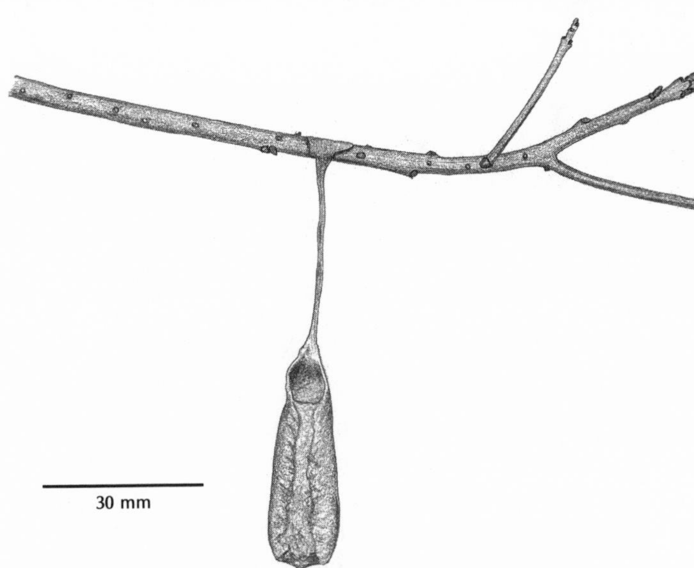


The cocoon of a promethea moth hanging on a sassafras twig.

Many animal patterns blend perfectly with the bark of trees. Since the texture as well as the color of bark is distinctive for each species of tree, you can often guess on which tree's bark certain animals can be found. By running their fingers over the ridges and grooves of the bark, some people can even identify certain trees with their eyes closed. Try it yourself. To small insects and mites, these ridges and grooves are part of a landscape in which hiding places abound where they can seek refuge. It is often a landscape where lichens and mosses sprout in scattered patches or cover large areas of the bark. As you look over this landscape with a magnifying glass, you may find a beetle or a bark louse meandering over hills and valleys of the bark. A moth or caterpillar may be nestled among the lichens.

The lichens on tree bark tell us about the air that we breathe. They are exceptionally intolerant of pollution and are one of the first life forms to disappear when air quality declines. Look over the bark of several different trees in your neighborhood to see how abundant lichens are. Remember that some trees, like beeches and white oaks, shed their dead bark quite rapidly, and lichens have little opportunity to get established on these trees. The bark of other trees, however, may be covered with a wide variety of lichens if the air is reasonably clear and free of pollutants.

1 mm

A bark louse that dwells in the lichen "forest."

# Living on a Leaf

In the few months between their unfurling in the spring to their fall in the autumn, leaves provide both room and board for a wide assortment of mites and insects. Some leaves are molded into galls or leaf rolls. Pieces of other leaves are taken by nibblers or leaf cutters. Sap is drained from some leaves by many sapsuckers. Leaves can obviously be generous hosts.

Sometimes the appetites of insects or the sheer numbers of insects become excessive. When leaf chewers start to destroy the leaves, trees make their hungry

A leaf beetle and its larva, which can expel a repellent from pairs of glands found on nine of its body segments.

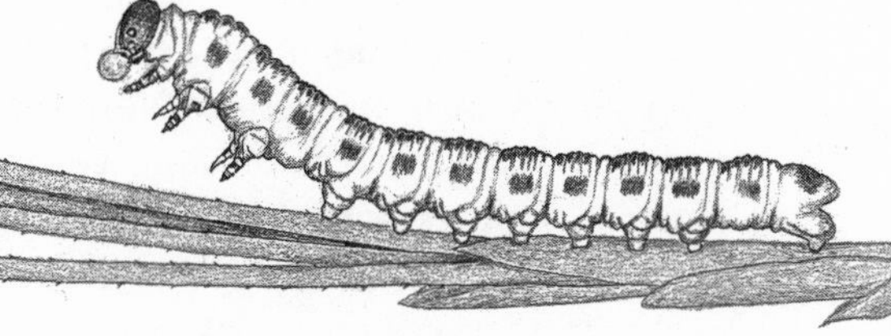

A sawfly larva expels a droplet of sticky repellent when it encounters a carpenter ant on white pine needles (leaves).

guests as unwelcome as possible. Sugars make leaves tasty, but other substances that leaves can produce to repel insects ruin the sugary flavor. Leaves can even warn each other that hungry insects are munching nearby. If leaves on one branch are rapidly being devoured, the leaves of a nearby branch or even a nearby tree will also start forming foul-tasting substances to ward off the approaching insects. The warning language of leaves is believed to be special chemicals given off by the chewed leaves. This chemical "message" is then passed on to leaves that are still untouched, and they are stimulated to produce repellent substances. Trees are certainly not defenseless when threatened by the jaws of caterpillars and other leaf chewers.

But for every repellent that a tree produces, there are certain insects that can break down the repellent substances or use these substances to their own advantage. Sawflies, which are relatives of hornets and horntails (pp. 64, 73), feed on pine needles as larvae and store a variety of noxious substances from pine resin in pouches near their mouths. When threatened by a predator, the sawfly larva rears its head and expels a sticky droplet of repellent from its mouth, sometimes even smearing the droplet on its attacker. Larvae of certain leaf beetles use the chemicals from leaves to produce their own repellent substances that they store in special glands found on most of their body segments. Whenever the larvae are disturbed, droplets of repellent ooze from each gland. And then there are other plant-eating insects that simply avoid contact with the unpleasant effects of the repellents that the leaves produce.

Most leaf-chewing insects, like caterpillars, get off to an early start in the spring before the trees' production of many disagreeable substances is in full swing. Young caterpillars start by taking very small bites from leaves. Immediately after the antlered caterpillar hatches from its egg on an oak leaf, it begins using each of its jaws like an ice cream dipper to scoop out the tender green portions of the leaf between the tougher and paler leaf veins. Only the skeleton of the leaf remains in the path of this little caterpillar. As the caterpillar grows, it sheds its antlers and its jaws become stronger. Soon it begins to devour entire leaves as it chews along.

Insects have found that leaves can be used for a number of purposes. Certain leaves are fashioned into various shapes and homes by insects known as leaf miners, leaf rollers, and case bearers. Even though these insects use their leaves as places to live, they still do not hesitate to eat a good portion of their homes.

Most caterpillars chew through all the layers of a

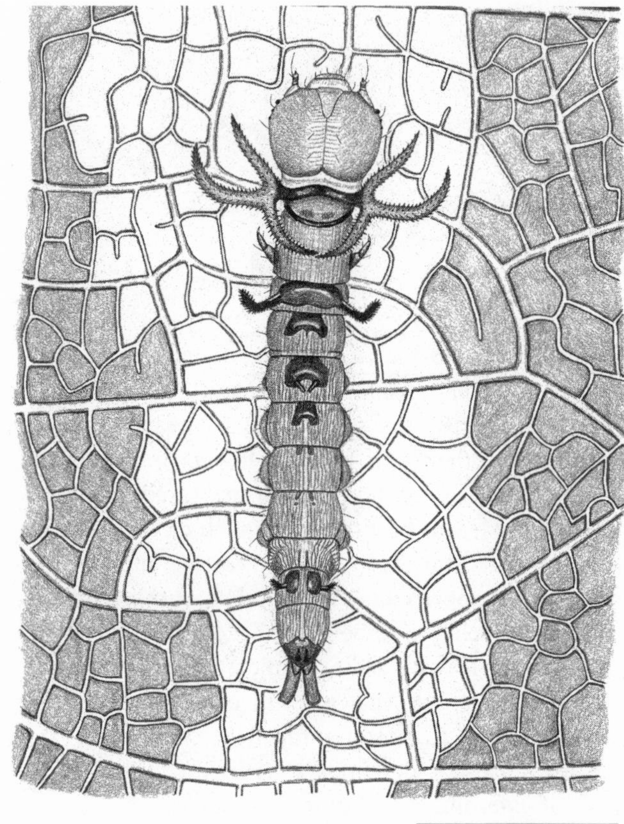


A young antlered caterpillar of a notodontid moth "skeletonizing" an oak leaf.

leaf. However, leaf-mining caterpillars eat only the soft, green tissue lying between the waxy layers on the top and bottom of a leaf, leaving these waxy layers as a roof and a floor. The miner then lives snugly between the two layers, first as a caterpillar and then as a pupa. When the miner finishes metamorphosis and is ready to fly off, it pokes its head through the roof of the mine and emerges as a very tiny moth. But caterpillars and moths are not the only ones that live in leaf mines. There are a few small, flat beetle grubs, fly maggots, and sawfly larvae that also mine leaves. Any creature is bound to be tiny that lives most of its life in the narrow space between the top and the bottom layers of a leaf.

Case-bearing caterpillars also mine leaves, but they live in cases that they construct from small pieces of leaves and only venture into their mines to chew on the tender tissues of the leaf. A tiny hole that they chew in the bottom layer of a leaf is both the entrance to and exit from the mine. Their cases are open at both ends. Like other leaf miners, they are neat about their house-keeping and back into their cases when they need to discard droppings from the rear openings of the cases. Case bearers move from leaf to leaf, mining during the summer. In the autumn they take their cases with them

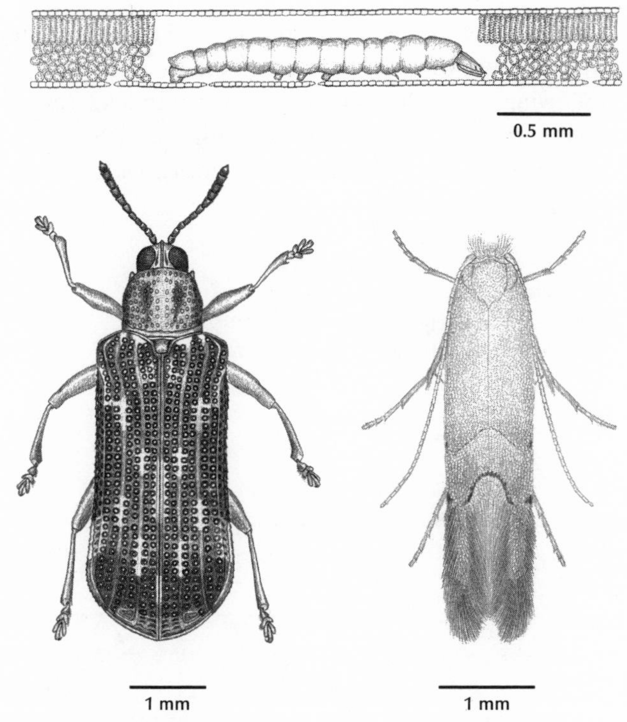


A leaf-mining caterpillar in its mine between the waxy layers of a leaf (*top*). A beetle (*left*) and a moth (*right*) whose larvae are leaf miners.

as they move to sheltered spots on the bark where they wait out the winter in their cases. As leaves appear the following year, the nearly grown caterpillars resume mining the new leaves until they retire to their cases in late spring to pupate and become moths. Different species of case-bearing caterpillars look very much alike, but their cases come in some distinctive shapes. Some cases look like snail shells; others look like pistols or cigars. Case bearers are better known for their unique cases than for any of their other attributes.

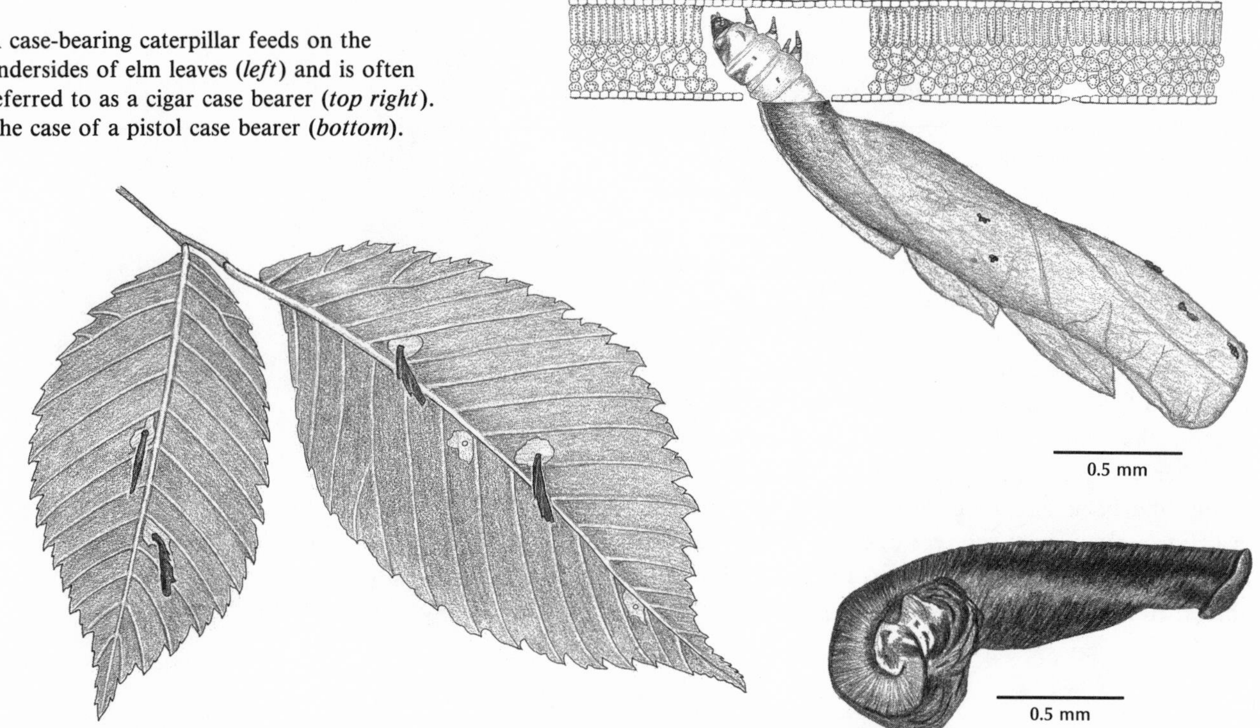


A case-bearing caterpillar feeds on the undersides of elm leaves (*left*) and is often referred to as a cigar case bearer (*top right*). The case of a pistol case bearer (*bottom*).

The basswood leaf roller needs a larger home than the one inhabited by a leaf miner or a case bearer. While still very small, this green caterpillar with a shiny black head makes a cut on one side of a basswood leaf and then begins rolling itself into the cut edge of the leaf. The caterpillar keeps the curled edge from unrolling by securing it with a few silken strands. In the privacy of its leaf roll, the caterpillar feeds until the time comes for it to transform into a moth.

A basswood leaf (*top*) with both a mine (light area between veins) and a portion of the edge rolled by a leaf roller. An adult moth (*bottom*) whose caterpillar is the basswood leaf roller.

The caterpillar of the even larger and more beautiful polyphemus moth consumes many leaves in its lifetime. If the polyphemus caterpillar is feeding on maple leaves, it probably consumes 40 or 50 leaves, but if it feeds on the smaller leaves of wild cherry, it can easily eat over a 100 leaves. All that eating is enough to carry it through both pupation and adulthood without its ever feeding again. You see, neither the pupa nor the moth of polyphemus has any mouthparts for chewing, biting, or sucking.

From the leaves that they consume, some female caterpillars extract and concentrate chemical scents, called pheromones, that they will use later as adults to attract male moths. The antennae of the males are so sensitive that they can detect the enticing odor of a female that may be many trees away.

Many insects spend their entire lives feeding on leaves. You can locate some of these insects, like the tree cricket, by listening for their chirps as they perch on the bark or on the tops of leaves, chirping and munching most of each day. On hot summer evenings, you can hear the high-pitched chirping of the male tree crickets in the treetops. To produce their chirps, they raise their wings and then rub them together vigorously. The

A polyphemus moth that has just emerged from its cocoon on a wild cherry twig.

tempo of chirping follows closely the rise and fall of the temperature. As summer progresses into autumn and evening temperatures drop, the boisterous chirping of the males fades into only feeble rattles. Of course, the chirping is not intended to inform you of the temperature, but to announce their presence to other crickets that listen with rather unusual ears. Cricket ears are not found in the usual place; you can find their ears just below the knees on their front legs.

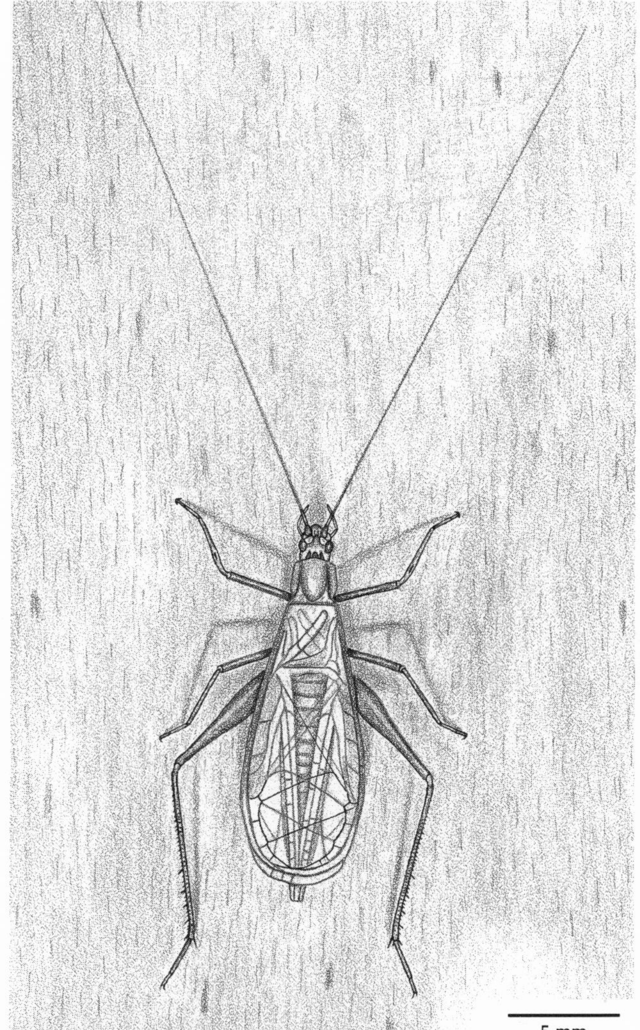


A male tree cricket on sycamore bark and an enlargement of its right front leg to get a closer view of a cricket's ear (*arrow*).

Female tree crickets are attracted to the males, not only by the sound of their chirping but by the scent or pheromone released from a gland that is exposed when the males raise their wings and begin chirping. The female crickets evidently appreciate males for their odors as well as their chirps.

Not all crickets that live in trees feed on leaves or sing from the treetops, however. A species of wingless cricket called the Carolina leaf roller lives inside leaves that it rolls. This cricket stays inside its roll during the day and then ventures forth at night to feed on aphids. Most crickets are musical leaf eaters but this one is a silent hunter.

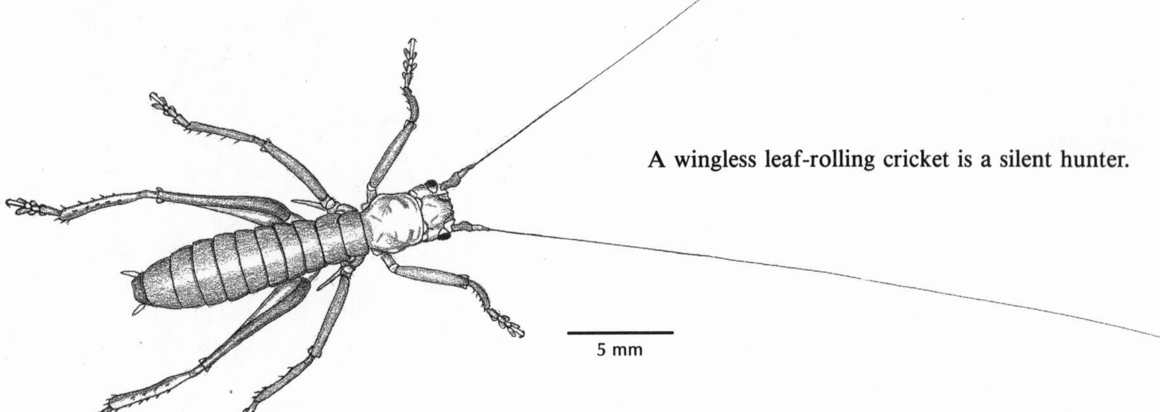


A wingless leaf-rolling cricket is a silent hunter.

Katydids also join in the music of the treetops on summer evenings. The males use their two wings to fiddle out their unmistakable song of "katydid." And every now and then they fiddle out "katy" and "katy didn't" to round off their repertoire. Female katydids' ears, one on each front leg below the knee, are tuned to these familiar refrains.

After being courted by the serenading males, female katydids go about their own matters in the treetops. They lay their pancake-shaped eggs in neat rows along twigs. After the leaves have fallen, the distinctive eggs are often easy to spot.

Tiny mites are other creatures that spend their entire lives feeding on leaves, and they can be found on the same twigs and leaves as the katydids. In fact, mites can be found just about everywhere—soil, ponds, household dust—so it should not be surprising that they are also found just about everywhere on trees. Because mites are so very tiny, you need to inspect a tree very carefully. A magnifier will help.

Pancake-shaped katydid eggs on an ash twig.

The easiest mites to find are probably the ones that live in little pouch-like galls on wild cherry and maple leaves. Each gall may have a family of 10 or more mites crowded inside, and each leaf can often be covered with over 100 galls. The number of gall mites on a single tree can easily add up to several million. Under a powerful microscope, these mites look like long cones with four short legs and a beak at one end. They are smaller than the period at the end of this sentence. They are so tiny

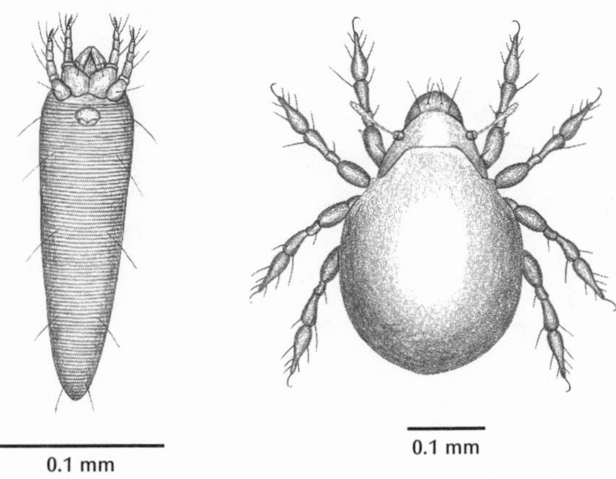


A mite that lives in a leaf gall (*left*), and a mite that lives on the underside of a leaf (*right*).

and colorless that you will have to take my word that they really do exist, unless you too have a powerful microscope and take the time to examine the inhabitants of a gall.

Other mites live on the underside of leaves and nestle into crevices found along the edges of large veins such as those of oak and hickory leaves. Mites come and go from their cozy shelters to feed on leaf sap or on other mites.

Mite galls come in different shapes. Spherical galls on silver maple leaves (*above*). Pencil-shaped galls on wild cherry leaves (*left*).

A katydid waving its long antennae as it prepares to sing.

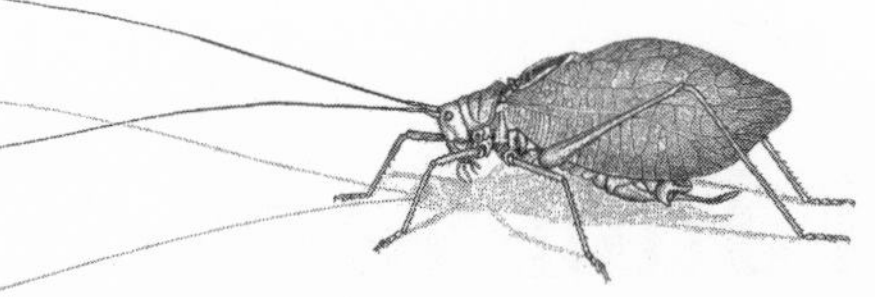


## LEARNING FROM TREES

While owls are flying silently through the dark, other flying creatures are moving about in the treetops. When a nearby light is switched on, beetles, tree crickets, katydids, and moths of almost every size, shape, and color will be drawn to the light. These flying insects that have come from their hidden worlds will parade in front of you, waving their antennae and flexing their jointed legs.

Another way to find out which moths and beetles are found in a forest is to entice them by "sugaring" with a tempting brew concocted of molasses, brown sugar, and stale beer. The proportions are not that critical as long as the brew is not too watery. Sugaring is an old trick that has been used by insect collectors for at least 200 years. On a warm summer evening, leave a trail of sugary patches on a number of tree trunks, logs, or fence posts. You will discover when you return to check your patches with a flashlight that beetles and moths of many colors and sizes will have found their way to the sweet-smelling treat.

Many insects—including aphids, katydids, and certain moths—pass the winter as eggs on bark and twigs. These eggs begin to hatch as soon as leaves begin unfolding in the spring and before the leaves have had a chance to produce many substances that repel insects. By getting an early start, these insects grow quickly on young, tender, untainted leaves.

Look for the egg masses of tent caterpillars before leaves appear on wild cherry or apple trees. The hundreds of eggs that make up the mass and encircle the twig are easy to spot on the bare twigs of winter trees. The newly hatched tent caterpillars build their silken tents only a few inches from their eggs. Look for the egg mass of the tent caterpillars in the figure on page 61.

Train your ears to listen for the music of cicadas, katydids, tree crickets, and tree frogs. In all cases, making music is strictly the province of males, and their songs really need to be heard to be remembered. Descriptions can only approximate the sounds that each species makes. The cicada drums out a prolonged "burr-r-r," and the katydid calls out its own name. Tree crickets and tree frogs sound the most alike. You might need a little practice to tell the tree cricket's "re-treat, re-treat" from the tree frog's trill. Creeping up on the musician with a flashlight may help verify your identification. The cricket or the frog will often be too intent on his music to notice your intrusion.

# Hunters and the Hunted

By enticing creatures to live on their leaves, bark, and flowers, trees also attract the predators that keep the numbers of these other creatures in check. Different wasps stalk and eat insects that feed on leaves and wood. Many songbirds flit from branch to branch in search of their six-legged meals. Nuthatches and woodpeckers constantly inspect the recesses of bark for any insects that may be sheltered there. Hawks and owls keep a sharp lookout for movements of birds and squirrels. Fishers search evergreens of the north woods for the scent of porcupines. The hunters and the hunted hold together the intricate web of life in a tree community.

A nuthatch on a hickory trunk.

# Wasps, Caterpillars, and Songbirds

A yellow-billed cuckoo eyeing tent caterpillars on a wild cherry branch.

Insects, like cicadas and stink bugs, that use their sharp beaks to dine on the sap of trees leave little trace of their presence except for an imperceptible hole here and there. But caterpillars and other leaf chewers are not such dainty eaters. Caterpillar trails are easy to follow from leaf to leaf; they leave their telltale signs—leaf rolls, leaf mines, and thoroughly chewed leaves.

During their daily routines, songbirds flit from branch to branch tracking down these caterpillars for breakfast, lunch, and dinner. And the caterpillars do their best to avoid these hungry birds. Some caterpillars have fuzzy coats that protect them from most birds, but there are a few birds whose appetites are not daunted by a little fuzziness. Cuckoos actually seem to prefer fuzzy caterpillars and can consume great numbers in a short time. During the daylight hours, when the birds are busiest searching the leaves for insects, many caterpillars retire to some silken web or dark and hidden nooks in the treetops. Here they wait until nightfall before venturing forth to munch on leaves. By this time most birds have gone to roost for the evening.

Although caterpillars may take cover from birds in leaf rolls or leaf mines, these hidden larvae can still be easily found by female ichneumon wasps. With their ultrasensitive antennae, these wasps can "smell" caterpillars that certainly have no special odor to our noses. The antennae seem to be in constant motion as they go about inspecting leaves and branches. Ichneumon wasps "sniff" for caterpillars on which to lay their eggs, for the body of the caterpillar provides food for their hungry, parasitic larvae.

Other wasps must also find caterpillars to feed their larvae. The eumenid wasps that nest in hollow twigs paralyze caterpillars and stash them in their nests. Their larvae can feast for many days on fresh caterpillar meat. Hornets, such as the bald-faced hornet, catch caterpillars and other insects, chew them, and then feed

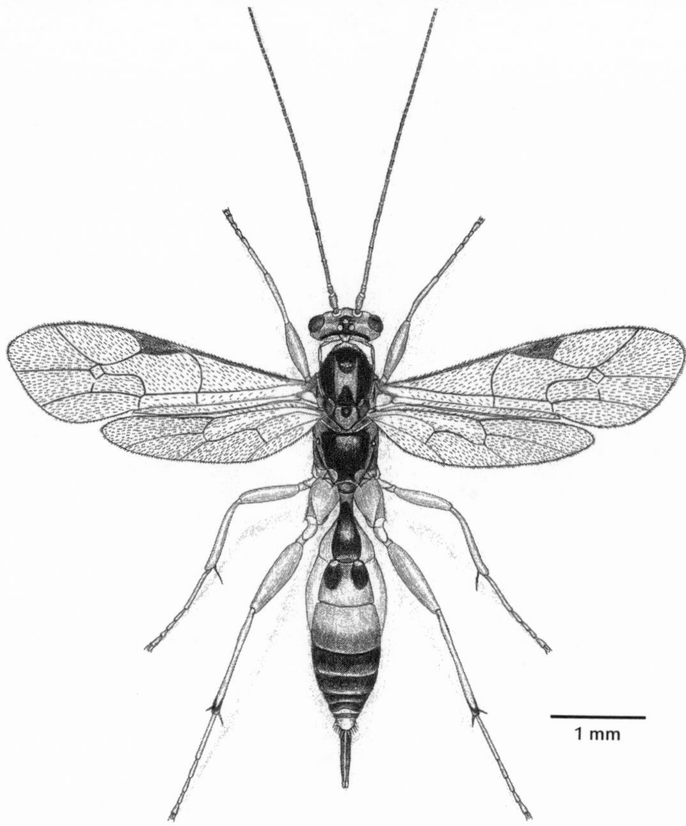


This ichneumon wasp parasitizes leaf-rolling caterpillars.

them to their large broods. As many as 20,000 hornets can live in one of their nests, beautifully crafted from chewed wood pulp. With that many hornets bustling around a tree, whatever caterpillars are around will not likely strip many leaves from that tree.

The hornet queen and her worker daughters do all the insect collecting as well as the pulp and paper making. Only at the end of the summer do male hornets begin appearing in the colony along with newly hatched queens. After the young queens have mated with the males, each queen finds a protected spot under bark or in a hollow limb where she can pass the winter. In the spring she begins the task of starting a new family and a new nest alone, for none of the males or workers survive the winter. She uses her jaws to scrape off bits of wood from tree trunks and limbs. She adds saliva, chewing the wood to a pulpy texture and shaping it into the foundation for a new nest. After the queen has constructed several brood chambers, she lays a fertilized egg in each one and then begins to nurse the daughter larvae that hatch from the eggs. Several weeks later all these larvae develop into workers that will build more brood chambers and nurse more larvae. But only the queen lays the eggs. Thanks to the assistance of her

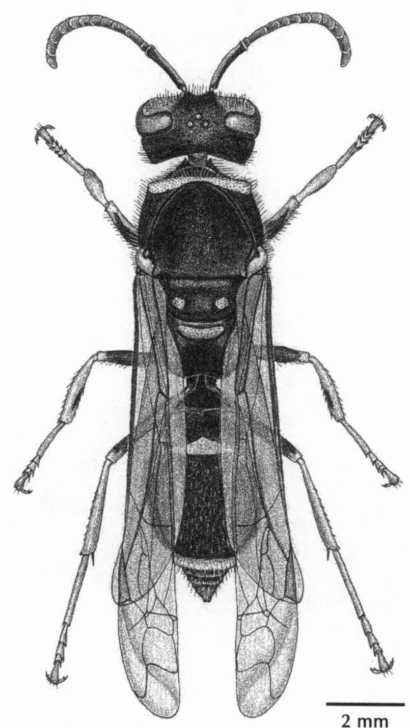


The eumenid wasp paralyzes its prey as food for its newly hatched larvae.

many daughters, the queen's nest grows from the few paper chambers she built first to several thousand brood chambers by the end of the summer.

The nest of bald-faced hornets on a maple branch.

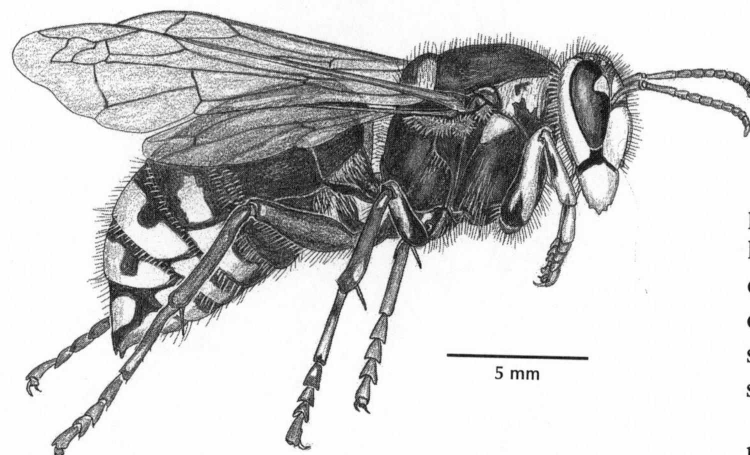


A bald-faced hornet out foraging.

You would suspect that hornets that have such painful stings would have few enemies, but even these hunters are also hunted. There are songbirds that not only share caterpillars with hornets, but they also feed on the hornets. Somehow birds such as tanagers can snatch hornets and bees from the air without ever being stung.

Even after caterpillars have finished feeding on leaves and have transformed into pupae and adults,

A scarlet tanager watching a hornet from a silver maple branch.

they are still tasty morsels for birds. In preparing for their transformation, some caterpillars climb down the tree to nestle in fallen leaves or to burrow into the soil. Others stay in the tree and masquerade as part of the tree—a leaf, a twig, a piece of bark. The pupa of the hackberry butterfly has a color pattern that not only blends with the green color of the hackberry leaf but also with the cream color of the leaf veins. Some caterpillars search for hiding places in the bark or in rolled leaves where they can quietly retire to pupate. But birds such as nuthatches and woodpeckers patrol tree trunks and routinely dig out insects from the recesses of the bark; jaunty vireos and warblers have an uncanny ability to find caterpillars tucked away in leaf rolls. The songbirds and their insect prey seem to constantly challenge each other in this game of hide and seek.

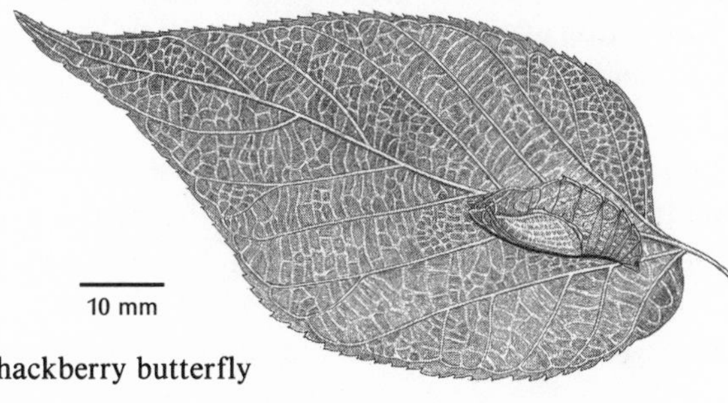


The camouflaged pupa of a hackberry butterfly on a hackberry leaf.

# Night Birds and Day Birds

A warbler, the common yellowthroat, seeking food on a willow branch.

Over 100 species of warblers travel north each spring as the number of insects rapidly grows and the hours of daylight rapidly increase. These active little birds scour every part of a tree in their pursuit of insects. While some species of warblers work the tops of the tallest trees, others hunt among the lower branches. Some species creep along tree trunks and poke about the bark for insects. A few warblers have even mastered the ability to catch insects on the wing.

After overwintering in Central and South America, vireos also head north each spring to nest in our forests. Vireos are the most abundant birds in many of the great forests and tiny woodlots found between the Atlantic coast and the Mississippi River. In late spring and early

A red-eyed vireo reaching for a caterpillar on the edge of a tulip tree leaf.

summer, they fill the trees with their exuberant and persistent singing while they hunt for their meals. Vireos might not be as varied in their colors and their habits as the warblers, but they have a reputation for weaving handsome, cupped nests that they suspend from forked branches.

At sunset, when vireos and other birds are return-

ing to the trees to roost, the owls of the forest are just setting out for an evening of hunting. Many roosting birds have ended their days in the talons and beaks of hungry owls. Nighttime raids on the roosts of other birds have made owls quite unpopular. However, if these other birds—especially jays or crows—ever come across an owl resting after one of its evening prowls, they get their revenge. The poor owl may have to endure their incessant scolding and harassment for many sleepless hours.

Crows harassing an owl on a bur oak limb.

# Fishers and Porcupines

Porcupines are particularly fond of buds, leaves, and bark of trees. Chewed trunks and branches in the treetops are telltale signs that you are in porcupine country of the north woods. Too many porcupines can easily overgraze the bark and buds of trees just as too many cattle can easily overgraze a pasture. Porcupines in a northern forest can get out of hand if their numbers

A porcupine (*below*) is not too sure about sharing the limbs of a white pine with a fisher (*above*).

are not kept in check by predators. Porcupines, however, are so well armed with spines that they shuffle through the trees with little concern for predators—except, that is, for relatives of weasels and skunks known as fishers. The fisher is one of the very few animals that is fast enough and agile enough to avoid the spines of porcupines. And after a meal of porcupine, the fisher leaves few scraps behind, not even the spines.

A tree provides not only the insects to feed a growing hornet colony but also the wood from which the paper nest is built. A hornet nest is lovely to behold. The interwoven strips of paper of many colors—oranges, browns, grays, yellows, and whites—represent the different kinds of trees and woody plants that were used in its construction. The paper was added layer by layer, hornet by hornet, each colored strip representing a mouthful of wood fibers gathered by a single hornet. Near a nest that is being constructed you may find a number of trees that show the scraping marks of the hornets' jaws. Remember that if you find a fully formed nest and want to see how it is constructed on the inside, do so only in the late winter or early spring, for it will then be empty. After all, you certainly do not want to confront a nest full of angry hornets. Besides being built with wood pulp rather than wax, the nests of hornets differ in other ways from those of honey bees. See if you can discover what some of these differences are.

Marks left by the jaws of hornets will only be a few millimeters wide, but teeth marks left by some of the larger tree dwellers like the porcupine may be several inches wide. You know you are in porcupine country if you find branches that have been chewed well above the reach of rabbits or beavers. Salt is a seasoning that porcupines are particularly fond of. You can probably persuade the porcupine to return for some more chewing by rubbing the chewed branches with some salt. You might catch it in the act the next time you return.

There are also a number of ways to become acquainted with some of the birds that visit trees around you. Using binoculars can help you get at least a few clear glimpses of some of the birds, but unless you attract them to a special spot, you may not see certain birds at all. To attract birds to your window or back porch, put out a bird feeder or a bird bath, or plant some trees like crabapples or dogwoods whose fruits are very tasty to birds. Birds will visit a feeder all year long. Some will even come to a bath in winter as long as the water does not freeze.

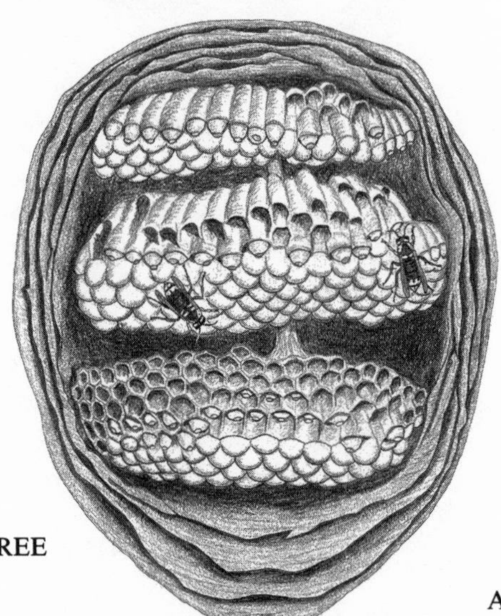

An inside view of a hornet nest.

A yellow-throated vireo and its distinctive nest in a wild cherry tree.

You can also get to know birds by the nests that they build, whether or not those nests are in trees. You will soon discover that birds that do nest in trees build their nests in tree cavities or in the crooks of branches, or they build hanging nests. Watch for nest-building activity. You might even record the progress of nest building with a camera. Using photography for nature study is a good way to improve your powers of observation as well as to learn a very rewarding hobby. Many nests that you fail to notice in the spring and summer may be more conspicuous on the leafless branches of winter trees. The nests that you locate in winter can also tell you where to look for certain birds in the coming year.

Birds communicate with their distinctive calls. By training your ears to recognize certain calls or the taps of certain woodpeckers, you can tell what bird is moving about in the leaves and branches overhead. There is a real satisfaction that comes from being able to figure out the identity of a bird you can not actually see.

Owls seem to have favorite trees on which to perch. If you ever come across one of these favorite perches, check the ground beneath for owl pellets. These are lumps of bones, fur, and feathers that are the size and shape of small, oblong cookies. After eating a bird or mouse, owls cough up the leftovers from their gizzards. The pellet is a record of the owl's hunting exploits. It may contain the fur of a mouse, the jawbone of a flying squirrel, or the brilliantly colored feathers of a songbird.

A barred owl perched in a cottonwood, watching for a meal.

# Hollow Twigs and Hollow Limbs

A dead limb is an inviting place. Even after its leaves are gone and its sap has dried, a dead limb has both food and lodgings to offer many creatures.

Wood borers are among the first animals to settle in a dead limb. Here, longhorn beetles and horntails lay eggs where their strong-jawed larvae can tunnel into the solid wood. Click beetle larvae prefer their wood a little more rotten and more tender. Wireworm is probably the better-known name for these long, thin, and hard larvae. The flat larvae of fire-colored beetles and buprestid beetles prefer living in the cramped quarters between the bark and dead wood of a limb. No wonder these larvae are so flat. Even though they never actually feed on wood, black carpenter ants (p. 49) carve extensive galleries through the wood and beneath the bark.

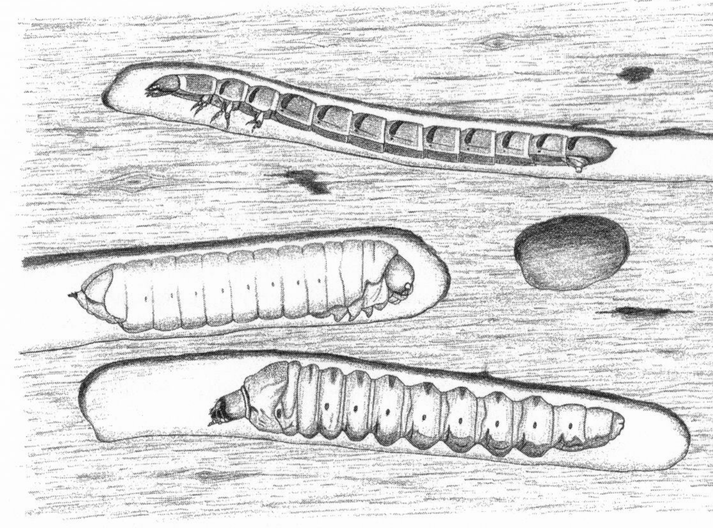

Larvae of a click beetle (*top*), a horntail (*middle*), and a longhorn beetle (*bottom*) tunneling in a dead limb.

5 mm

Dead limbs seem to have accommodations for wood borers of many different tastes and many different forms.

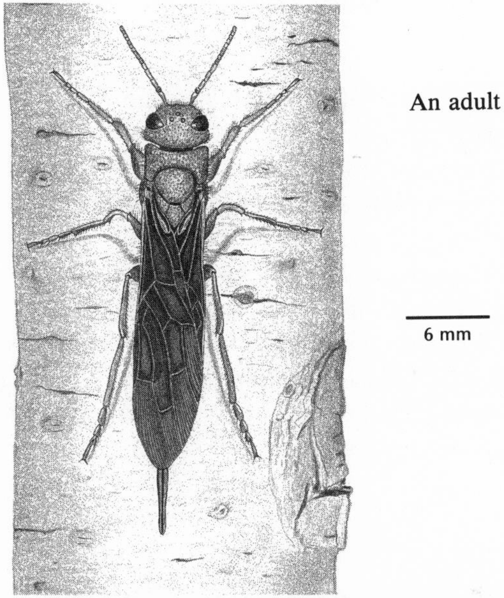

An adult horntail.

6 mm

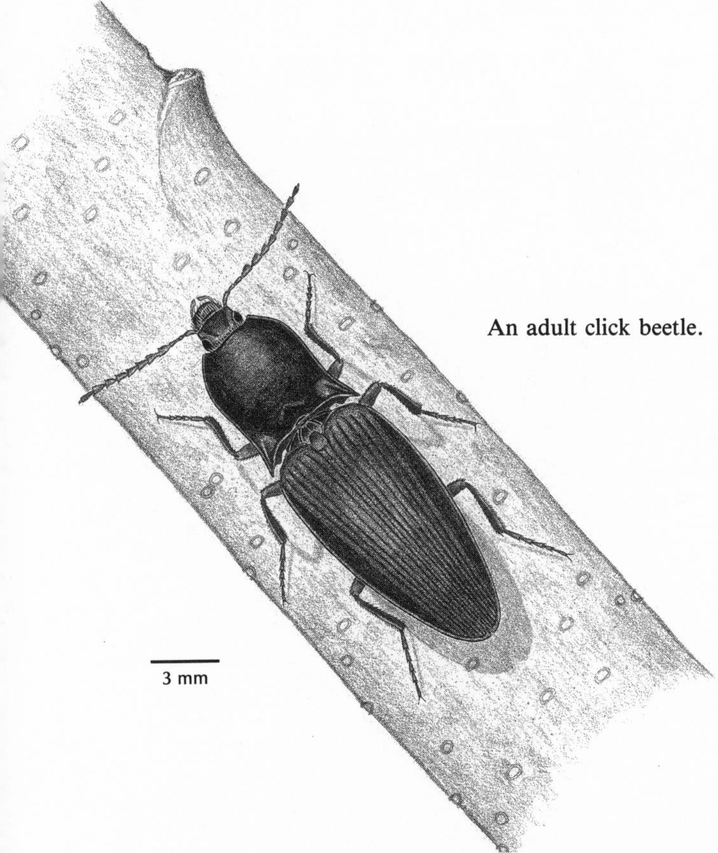


An adult click beetle.

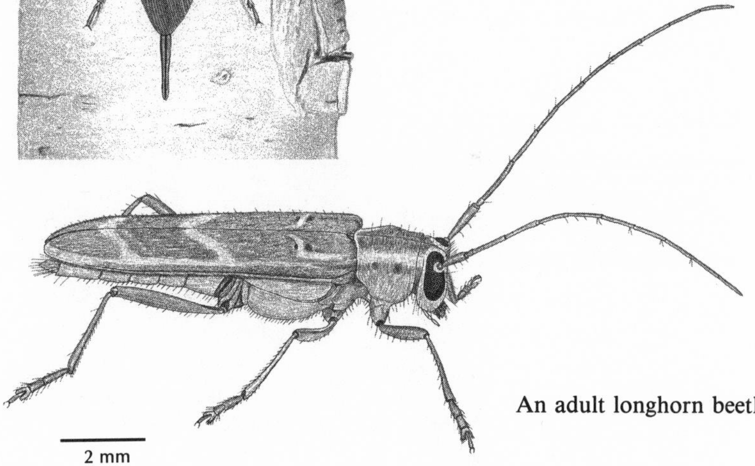

An adult longhorn beetle.

2 mm

Whether the wood of a dead limb is solid or rotten, however, wood fibers alone are not particularly nourishing to the insects that live there. But fungi and bacteria also live in tunnels that permeate the wood and these are quite tasty and nutritious to wood-boring insects. Also, certain bacteria and microscopic single-celled animals called protozoans dwell in the guts of many wood-boring insects and actually digest the tough wood fibers for their hosts as well as for themselves.

The lives of different wood-boring insects are spent mainly as larvae, chewing tunnels through wood. After navigating through the wood, sometimes for more than a year, the larvae finally stop chewing and begin their metamorphosis. As their wings develop and then unfurl, horntails and beetles leave their dark tunnels for life above the bark.

Even though the wood borers lie hidden in their dark tunnels, they can still fall victim to birds and ich-

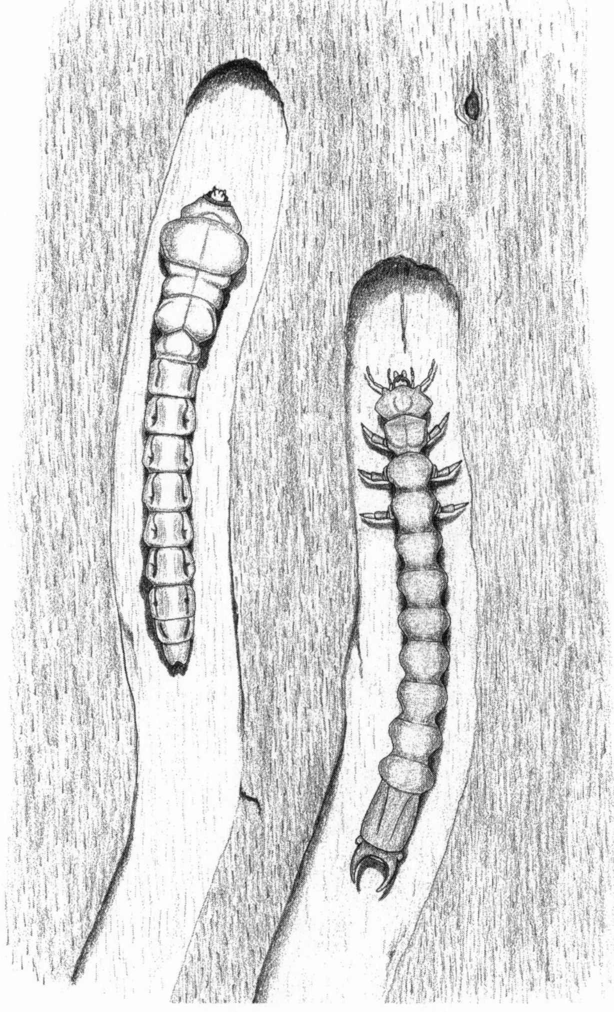

Larvae of the fire-colored beetle (*right*) and the buprestid beetle (*left*) under the bark of a red oak.

5 mm

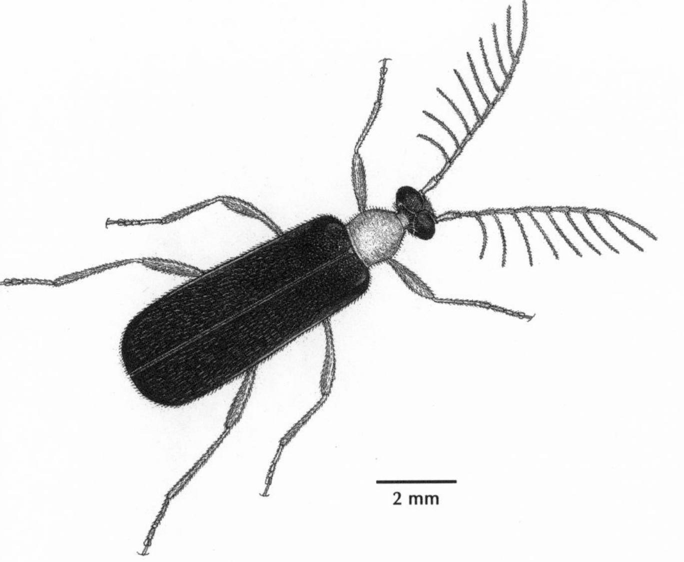


An adult fire-colored beetle.

neumon wasps. Using their very sensitive antennae, female ichneumon wasps always manage to find some hidden larvae on which to lay the eggs that hatch into their own parasitic larvae. The ovipositors of certain ichneumon wasps are much longer and stiffer than those of the wasp (p. 62) that parasitizes leaf-rolling caterpillars. With ovipositors that can be several inches long, the wasps drill through bark and wood to reach larvae lying in tunnels deep within.

An adult buprestid beetle.

2 mm

A downy woodpecker outside its nest hole in a willow.

Woodpeckers also investigate and peck at a limb that promises to have some wood borers inside. Caterpillars are in season for only a few months each year, but wood borers are a year-round source of food. Although the borers may not be very active on cold days, woodpeckers can still find them as easily in the winter as they can in the summer. The holes that one woodpecker starts as it searches for larvae may be enlarged by other woodpeckers and may eventually end up as one big hole for still another woodpecker's nest.

Woodpeckers and wood borers are not the only ones that live in tree holes. Flying squirrels, nuthatches, and even some larger birds settle into secondhand woodpecker holes. The flying squirrels and nuthatches use strips of fine bark, a little grass, and a few leaves to pad their nests. Wood ducks line their nests with their down feathers. Great crested flycatchers line their tree cavities with any number of materials—bark, twigs, hair, feathers. And for some reasons known only to the flycatchers, they also habitually add snake skins to their nests. Bluebirds haphazardly add a few grasses and weeds, but sparrow hawks (also called kestrels) do not bother to add any bedding of their own.

While the birds use the big holes, leaf-cutting bees and eumenid wasps (p. 63) sometimes move into the vacant tunnels of horntail or longhorn beetle larvae. Once these bees and wasps locate a hollow twig or hole left by a wood borer, they set out to remodel it, each in its own special way. They are more fastidious about their nests than the birds are about theirs.

Without a ruler or compass, the bees are able to bite off perfectly circular pieces of leaves just the right size and shape to build a series of leafy chambers in the tunnels left by wood borers. In each chamber the bees store a good supply of nectar and pollen before laying an egg. The chambers are then sealed with more round pieces of leaves.

Eumenid wasps use mouthfuls of mud to build chambers in hollow twigs for their larvae. Like other wasps—and unlike the bees—these black and yellow wasps provide insects as food for their larvae. A mother wasp will stash just enough paralyzed caterpillars in each nursery chamber to nourish a larva from the time

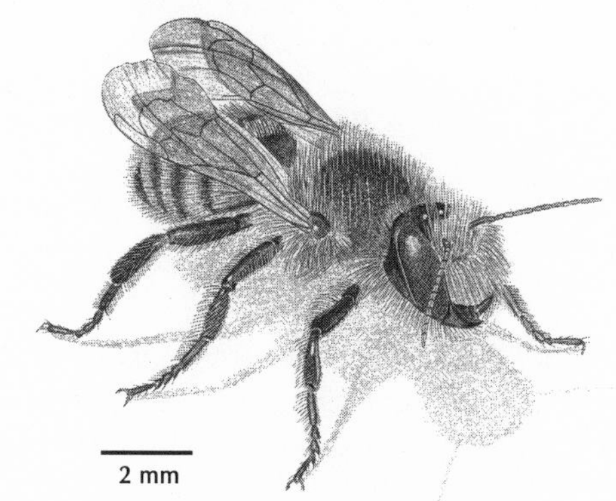

A leaf-cutting bee and its distinctive circular holes in redbud leaves.

A flower fly inspecting a tree hole pool before laying eggs.

it hatches until the time it undergoes metamorphosis. After the caterpillar and egg are in place, the female wasp neatly seals off each chamber with a thin wall of mud.

Some tree holes act as basins for rainwater. Many insects and mites quickly populate the tiny pools of water where they are safe from the jaws of fishes and frogs. Creatures that live in these basins feed on either debris in the hole or on creatures smaller than themselves. Many beetles, flies, and mosquitoes return generation after generation to these pools to lay their eggs.

In many forests, tree holes that are filled with rainwater are few and far between. Even though the water often becomes unsavory, these pools are especially coveted by a number of interesting creatures. Flower flies (also called syrphid flies) are among those insects that search for the scarce, rain-filled holes. Once a male flower fly discovers one, he guards it diligently until a female fly joins him. By looking and sounding like bumble bees, flower flies also guard against hungry birds and tree frogs. After the fly eggs hatch, the maggots inherit the tree hole from their parents. These rat-tailed maggots have a unique way of breathing as they feed and move about in the debris at the bottom of the pool. An air tube in the tail acts as a telescoping snorkel that can stretch several inches or shrink to less than an inch.

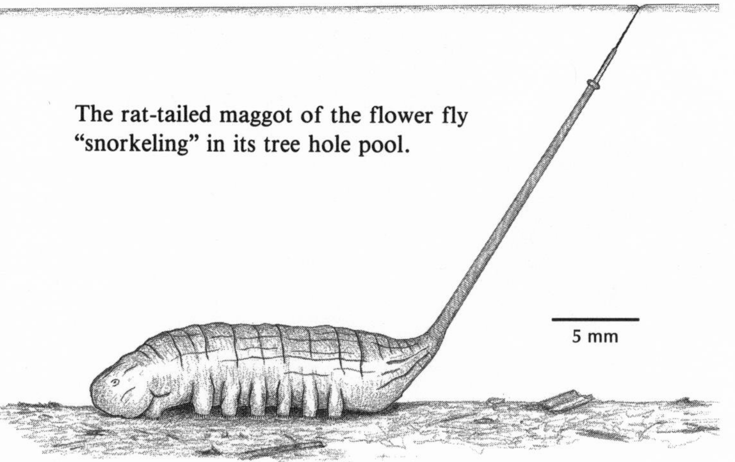


The rat-tailed maggot of the flower fly "snorkeling" in its tree hole pool.

In their old age, trees become the dominion of borers and woodpeckers, owls and raccoons, and even some flies and their maggots. Even though their roles may change, old trees, like old people, can continue to be productive and useful members of their communities.

## LEARNING FROM TREES

In the dark and sheltered world beneath the bark of dead limbs, you will come across some creatures that spend most of their lives on the underside of the bark. They seem well suited for living in the darkness and dampness. With a pocketknife, slowly and carefully pry loose a piece of bark to get some idea of what goes on in this part of a tree. Why are these creatures shaped as they are? What do they feed on here in the darkness? What will they become? After you have satisfied your curiosity, show respect for the creatures that live under the bark and gently replace any bark that you may have removed.

Reading the tracks left by the engraver beetle beneath the bark can tell you about the family life of these insects. When the mother beetle finds a branch where she can lay her eggs, she first drills through the bark and then carves a trough called the brood gallery. Here she distributes her eggs and when the larvae hatch, each gnaws into the wood and leaves a trail that radiates from the central gallery. Somehow, each larva steers a course between the trails being gnawed nearby by its brothers and sisters. Their trails neither cross nor collide. At the end of its trail, the larva pupates. When the adult beetle emerges, it drills its way to the surface of the bark. Each artistic, patterned engraving that you see beneath the bark is the work of an entire family of engraver beetles.

The rich community of life on a tree is lessened each time a dead limb or hollow trunk is removed. As these trees and limbs are cleared from a forest or wooded

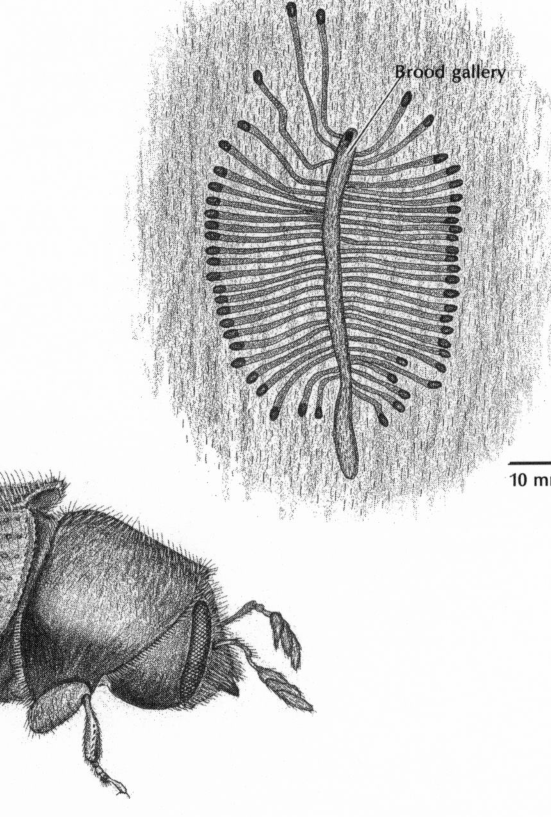


The engraver beetle and her brood galleries.

street, many birds are deprived of housing and a rich source of food. Not only will woodpeckers move out of the neighborhood, but other birds like screech owls, sparrow hawks, wood ducks, and bluebirds must also seek other tree holes where they can nest. You can encourage these birds to stay around a neighborhood that has a shortage of hollow limbs by providing nest boxes. Many birds will build their nests and raise their families even though the wood borers and fungi that normally share their hollow limbs are missing from the unpainted lumber of the nest boxes.

One basic plan for a nest box has been designed that will suit many birds; for different species of birds, just use different dimensions (see table below). Before hang-

DIMENSONS OF NEST BOXES FOR DIFFERENT SPECIES OF BIRDS

| | Bird | | | | | |
|---|---|---|---|---|---|---|
| | Wood duck | Sparrow hawk | Screech owl | Great crested flycatcher | Bluebird | Nuthatch |
| *Dimensions of nest box* (inches) | | | | | | |
| **Length*** | 18 | 16 | 14 | 10 | 9 | 9 |
| **Width*** | 14 | 10 | 8 | 6 | 5 | 4 |
| **Height*** | 14 | 10 | 10 | 7 | 6 | 7 |
| **Diameter*** | 4 | 3 | 3 | 2 | 1½ | 1¼ |
| *Height of nest box aboveground* (feet) | 10–20 | 10–30 | 10–30 | 8–20 | 5–10 | 12–20 |

*See figure of birdhouse.

A sparrow hawk (kestrel) prefers the natural hole in this walnut tree but may also settle into a nest box.

ing nest boxes for sparrow hawks or wood ducks, add 2–3 inches of woodchips or coarse sawdust to the floor. Since fledgling wood ducks must be able to climb to the opening of the nest box, there should be a piece of hardware cloth placed between the floor of the nest box and its opening. This will act as a ladder for the young ducks. Remember, too, if your nest box is for wood ducks, it must be placed near a pond, lake, or marsh. You can use nails for assembling most of the nest box, but you should use brass wood screws to attach the top. Each autumn the top can then be detached and old nest materials removed. As the final step, choose a good location and attach the nest box securely to a limb or tree trunk with a strong rope that passes through both holes in the back board.

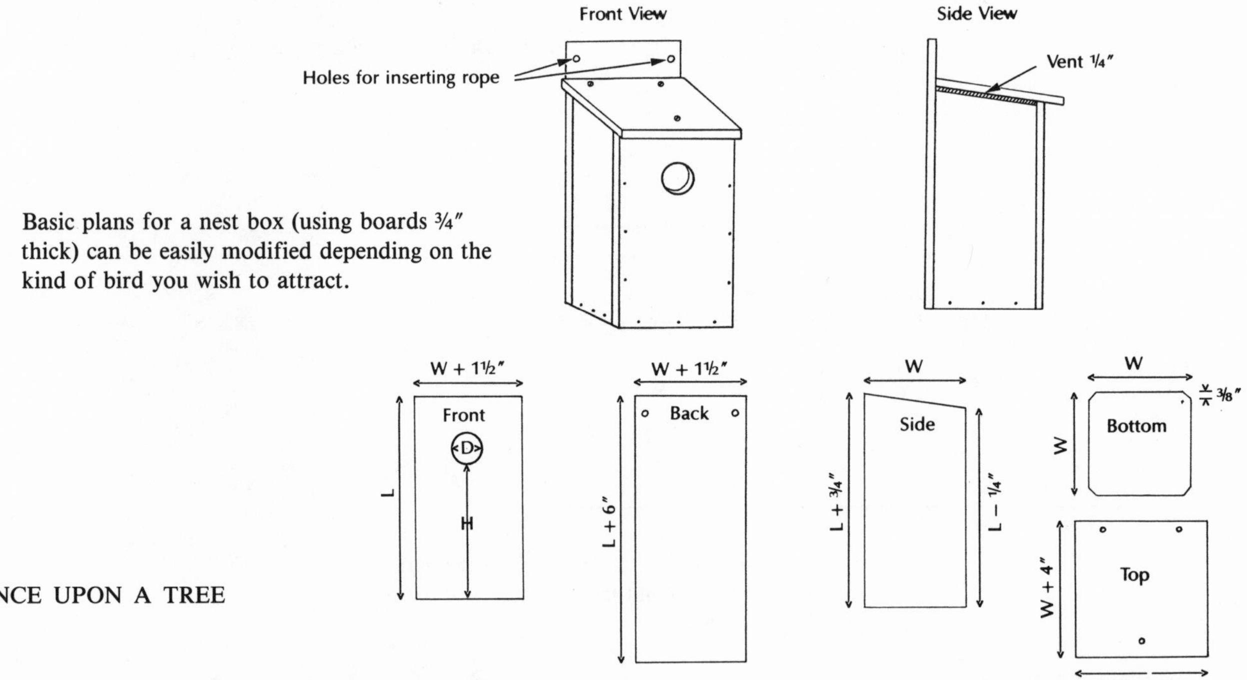


Basic plans for a nest box (using boards ¾″ thick) can be easily modified depending on the kind of bird you wish to attract.

The loss of old limbs and old trees from an area not only deprives the birds of spring and summer housing but certain insects are also left without winter shelter. Hollow limbs and tree trunks are often winter homes for hornet queens, stink bugs, and ladybird beetles. There are also a few moths as well as butterflies that overwinter as adults. These include the well-known mourning cloaks, question marks, commas, and red admirals (p. 11). Carefully search a hollow trunk with a flashlight on a cold winter day for some of these insect hibernators.

After spending their evenings soaring over the treetops in search of whatever flying insects may be out, bats retire to hollows in trees during the day. Look for their fast-moving silhouettes in the evening sky. To be sure the silhouette is that of a bat and not a bird, toss a small stick or twig in the air toward it (NOT directly at it) and see if the figure chases it through the air. Birds will usually ignore flying sticks, but bats will quickly change course to pursue whatever flies past them.

Bats are not only enjoyable to watch as they fly acrobatically through the evening sky, but they also help to keep down the number of flying insects. A single bat can eat several thousand insects each night. These include moths as well as mosquitoes and midges from the tree holes. If old hollow trees are uncommon where you live, you can encourage bats to move into your neighborhood by placing bat houses about 12–15 feet aboveground on

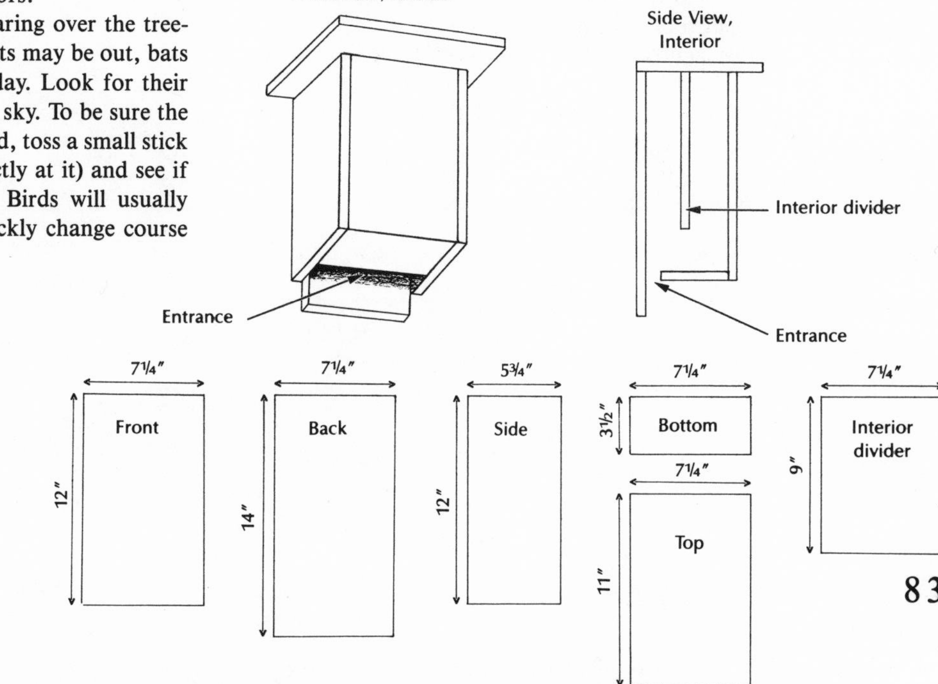


Basic plans for a bat house.

the east sides of trees or houses with clear access to the entrances. A bat house is simple to build from lumber. Follow the plan for making a bat house; with a chisel or knife roughen the surfaces of the boards that will face the inside so the bats can easily climb on them. Also, stain or paint the outer surfaces of the boards a dark color so the house will absorb heat from the sunlight. Bats prefer warm houses made from rough boards, but they may not find the house you build for a year or two. Be patient! When the bats leave in the autumn, butterflies and other insects may move in for the winter.

Most squirrels travel about trees during all hours of daylight, but the tiny flying squirrel does not leave its den in a hollow limb or trunk until dark. If flying squirrels are around, they are very likely to visit your bird feeder some evening, especially if the feeder is stocked with sunflower seeds, various nuts, or pieces of fruit.

Another mammal that is likely to set out from its nest in a hollow tree and pay an evening visit to your bird feeder is the white-footed mouse. Its long whiskers and its sensitive nose guide this little hunter to the insects, seeds, and fruit that are found at the feeder or on the tree.

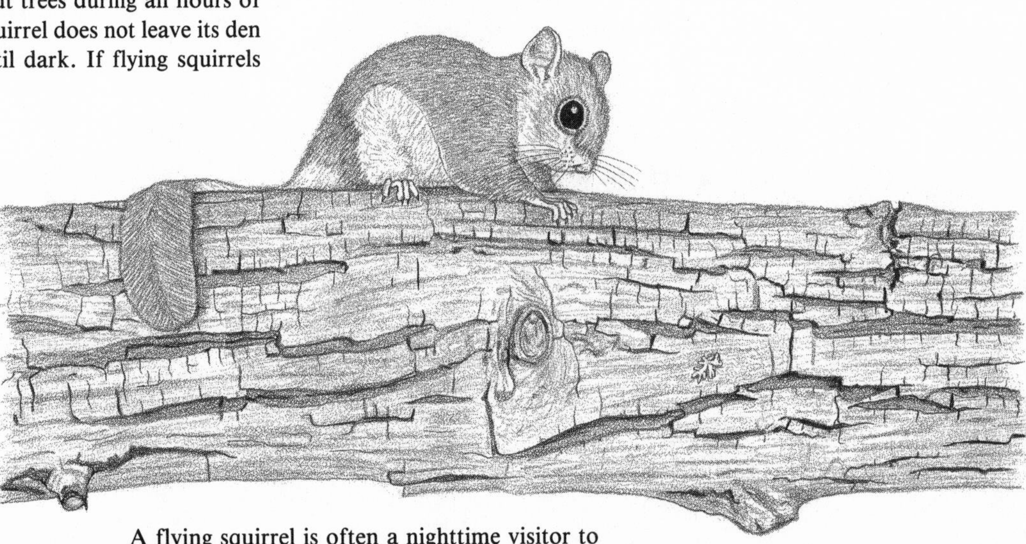

A flying squirrel is often a nighttime visitor to bird feeders.

A white-footed mouse often dines on seeds it has raided from a bird feeder.

Larger tree dwellers like raccoons, possums, and porcupines may also appear at your feeder. In the woods and country as well as in some towns and cities, you can look for their tracks, which may suddenly end at the base of a tree. These tracks are especially easy to spot when snow is on the ground. Old, hollow trees may be ideal places for them to settle down when they are not wandering about in search of food. On a hot afternoon in July, I once discovered that a raccoon was watching me from the shade of its den tree as I walked through a city park. Keep an eye out for such old, hollow trees where other eyes may be watching you.

Raccoon

White-footed mouse

Tracks you may see near a hollow tree.

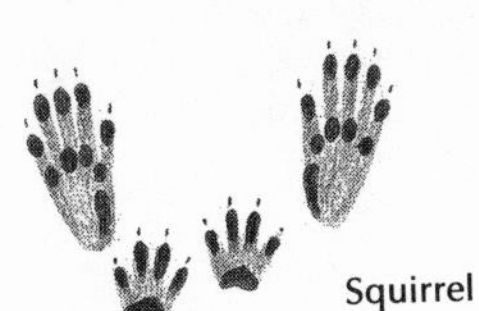

Squirrel

Porcupine

Possum

50 mm

# Planters and Harvesters

We know that many trees rely on their animal inhabitants to disperse and plant their seeds. Even though our knowledge of these natural events seems vast, we are still learning how different members of a tree community rely on one another in ways that we never imagined.

In the early 1970s on the tiny island of Mauritius in the Indian Ocean, people noticed that none of the lofty dodo trees on the island was younger than 290 years old. No trees had sprouted since about 1680. That date closely corresponded to the year when the large flightless birds, also called dodos, last walked the island and became extinct. Was this simply coincidental or were the dodo birds in some way responsible for the sprout-

A gray squirrel seeking acorns in red oak leaves.

ing of the dodo trees? We shall never know for certain how or if the lives of these birds were linked with the lives of the trees, but we can find out if a close relative of the dodo bird, the turkey, can take the place of its extinct relative. Seeds from dodo tree fruits do not sprout on their own, but they sometimes sprout after they have been swallowed by a turkey and then passed in its droppings. The tough seed coat is apparently scratched, or scarified, just enough by the grinding action of a turkey's gizzard to let the first root break through and establish its foothold in the soil. It is probably a safe guess that a trip through the gizzard of a dodo bird was once a route traveled by every dodo tree of Mauritius.

Think about all the oak trees that have gotten their start in this world, thanks to those industrious, but forgetful, squirrels. Every autumn squirrels rustle among the fallen leaves, gathering and burying acorns for the cold days that lie ahead. Somehow, a good portion of those buried acorns never get found again. Many will sprout and grow into oaks of the forest.

Blue jays also hoard acorns during the autumn harvest. And like the squirrels, the jays can be forgetful. They may forget that they ever buried some acorns miles away in a forest clearing or in an old pasture.

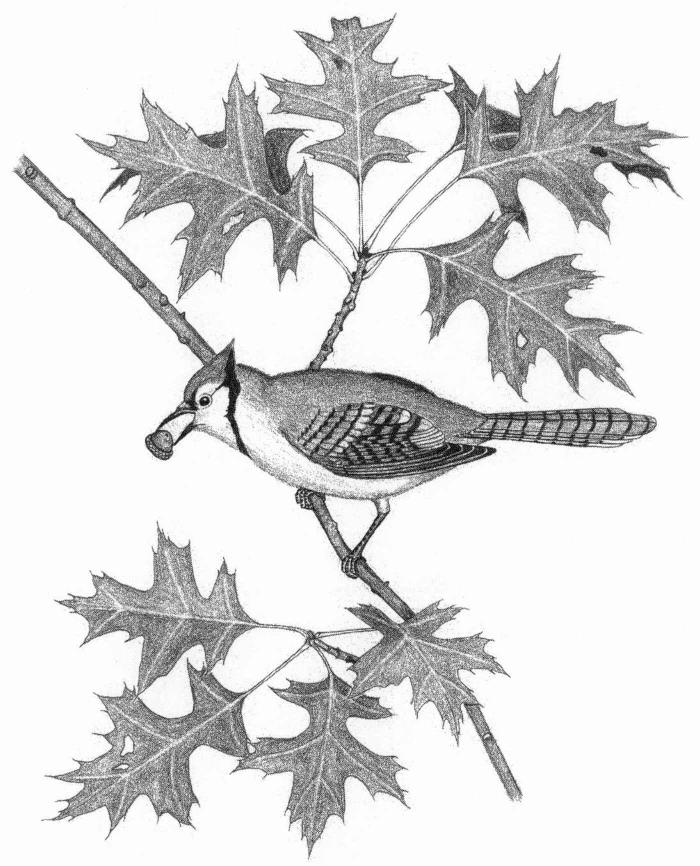

A bluejay with a pin oak acorn.

They unintentionally find new homes for oak trees and reforest the landscape.

Each autumn thousands of acorns fall from a single oak tree, and each year a few of these are claimed by acorn weevils. Before the acorns start to fall, the female weevil chooses the acorns in which she will lay her eggs. She uses the tiny jaws at the tip of her long snout to drill a hole in each acorn, and then she drops an egg inside each one. The little white grub that hatches grows fat inside its acorn nursery. When the acorn falls from the oak in an autumn wind, the full-grown grub leaves its nursery and burrows into the ground to pupate and spend the winter.

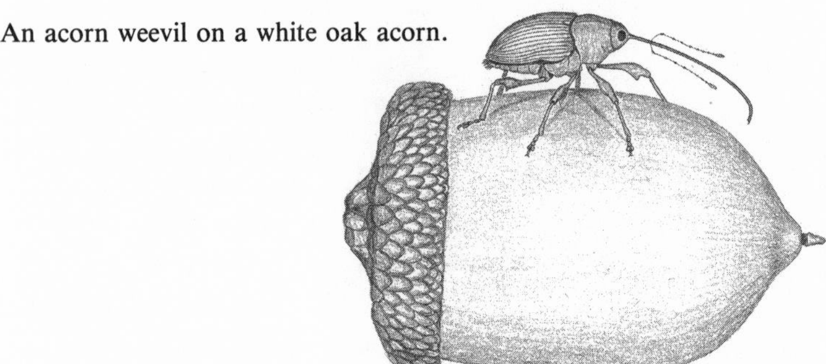


An acorn weevil on a white oak acorn.

The harvest of an oak tree is so bountiful that weevils, blue jays, and squirrels can all claim a share of acorns and there will still be plenty remaining to sprout into new trees.

Walnuts and squirrels also have a good partnership. Wind and birds may scatter seeds of many trees, but squirrels are usually the only ones who scatter the tough and bulky walnuts. For all these hard-shelled nuts that squirrels manage to chew into, they probably bury just as many in the soil each autumn. Each spring walnut seedlings appear, often far from the tree where they fell.

Another creature helps squirrels with their walnut harvest. When the walnuts fall from a tree, each is covered with a firm, green husk. This husk and the hard shell of the walnut provide obstacles to squirrels trying to chew their way to the tasty nut within. But the husk is just what appeals to the walnut husk fly. Male and female flies meet, court, and mate on the surface of the husk. The maggots that hatch from the eggs the females leave behind chew through the husk until it almost disintegrates and readily falls away. The maggots then crawl out and burrow into the soil where they wait out the winter months. Now, thanks to the maggots, the walnuts can be easily husked and the squirrel can go about chewing through the shells and harvesting the nuts.

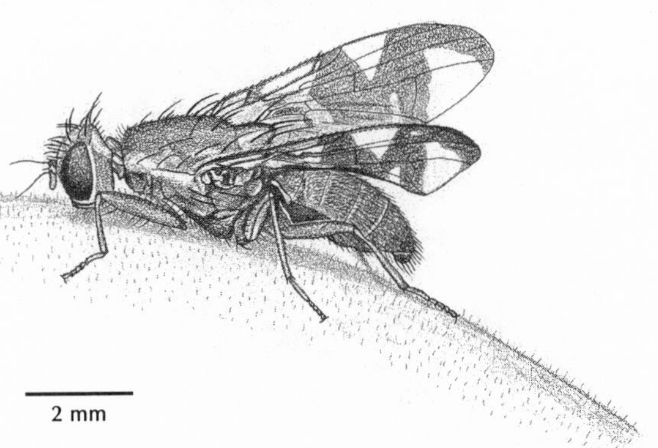

After walnuts have fallen, persimmons will soon follow. Raccoons, possums, and foxes all love persimmons. They devour the whole fruit—skin and pulp as well as seeds. In October, the animals' trails are marked with droppings that are peppered with persimmon seeds. For this reason, many persimmon trees probably line the routes of animal trails that have been used for many years. Having persimmon trees growing by the sides of these trails is a good arrangement for animals and trees alike. The animals have a ready source of sweet fruit, and the trees have plenty of volunteers to scatter their seeds abroad.

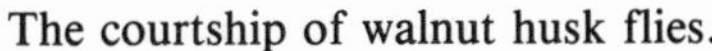
The courtship of walnut husk flies.

Tasty persimmons beckon this raccoon.

Each fall before the persimmon harvest, waves of migrating birds sweep across the country as their instincts to migrate are awakened by the longer nights and cooler days. During the long flight southward, each bird must meet the energy needs of its demanding travel schedule. With the arrival of autumn, the ripening fruits of trees are now a more plentiful source of energy than the few insects that are left at the end of summer. Fruits of dogwood, sassafras, and tupelo are rich in fats and provide birds with more calories for their demanding flights than fruits that are sweet with sugars. Mammals like raccoons and possums prefer the sweet fruits of persimmons and wild cherries, leaving the fat-laden fruits for the migrating birds. As the fatty fruits ripen, the leaves on these trees turn bright orange and red as though to advertise their location to birds flying high overhead. Migrating birds relish the fruits and harvest them all in a matter of days. Where the bird droppings fall, new trees will someday sprout and eventually nourish yet another generation of birds that passes the same way.

## LEARNING FROM TREES

From late August through October, acorns, walnuts, and other fruits begin falling to the ground. A number of these will be homes for larvae of beetles, moths, and

A migratory wood thrush eyeing the ripe, red fruits on a dogwood branch.

flies. As the days of autumn shorten and before the air becomes too chilly and the ground becomes well frozen, these larvae leave their homes to migrate down to the leaf litter and soil where they will pupate. Nuts and fruits that you collect early in the fall are likely to still have an assortment of larvae inside. Place some of the fruits and nuts in a covered container with an inch or two of loose, moist soil. Before temperatures drop below freezing, place your container in a box partly buried in the soil or under a pile of leaves to protect the pupae from extreme temperatures. After being outdoors through the winter, the pupae will transform into adults the following spring.

To see just how hard the squirrels have to work to get at the walnut meat and to appreciate the role of the husk flies, try husking and cracking a walnut that has just fallen from a tree. To get an idea of how effective a squirrel is as a planter of trees, bury several walnuts or acorns an inch or two in the soil and see how many of these nuts sprout the following spring.

Try sampling fruits from a variety of trees. Sweet fruits like apples, cherries, persimmons, and plums are rich in sugars. Fruits of dogwood, tupelo, and sassafras may be rather bitter so only take a nibble, but these fruits are excellent sources of energy. Gram for gram and ounce for ounce, they provide more energy from their fats than the sweet fruits ever provide from their sugars. Migrating birds take advantage of this energy value.

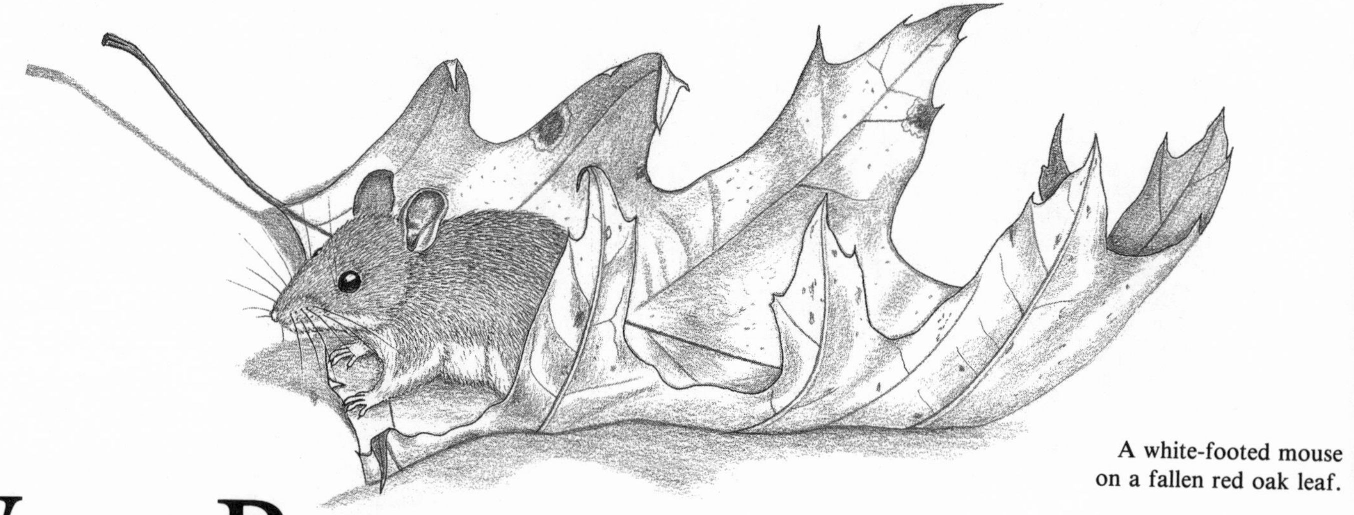

A white-footed mouse
on a fallen red oak leaf.

# Winter's Rest

After the harvest of nuts and fruits, leaves settle to the earth just as they did on the autumn day in 1853 when Thoreau wrote about them in his journal.

How pleasant to walk over beds of these fresh, crisp, and rustling fallen leaves. . . . How beautiful they go to their graves! They that waved so loftily, how contentedly they return to dust again and are laid low, resigned to lie and decay at the foot of the tree and afford nourishment to new generations of their kind. . . . How they are mixed up, all species—oak and maple and chestnut and birch! They are about to add a leaf's breadth to the depth of the soil. We are all the richer for their decay.

Life moves at a slower pace now. The warblers, vireos, and thrushes have flown south, but the mammals and many of the birds remain. They leave their telltale tracks in the snow. From their rich harvest of fruits and nuts, they store extra fat in their bodies to sustain them through the cold days that lie ahead. With the shorter days of autumn, the insects enter a resting state known as diapause. Diapause is a state of slowed activity and arrested development. The development of overwintering eggs and immature insects is temporarily halted, as is reproduction of the few insects that overwinter as adults. Also, some of the overwintering adults change color. Adult lacewings change from green to reddish brown to match the color of the dead leaves in

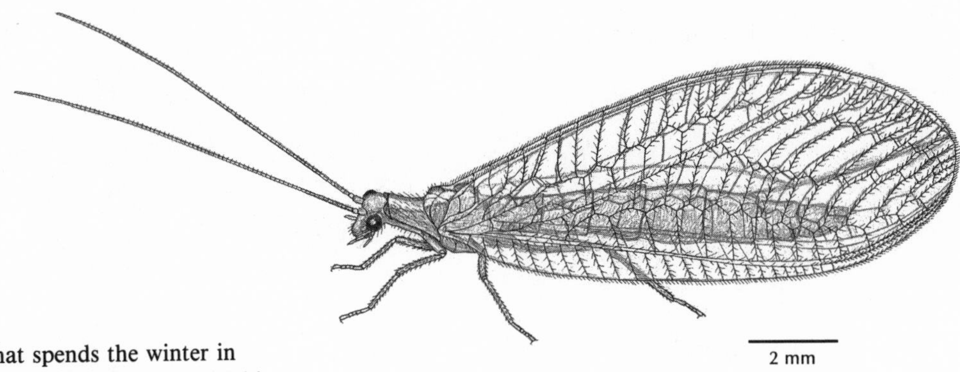


An adult lacewing that spends the winter in fallen leaves looks too fragile to survive frigid temperatures.

which they spend the winter. During autumn, insects produce and store chemicals in their blood that will act as antifreeze. At last all preparations have been made for surviving the rigors of winter. Only after they have been exposed to several weeks of frigid temperatures will the warmer temperatures and longer days of spring break the diapause of insects.

When the coldest days of winter arrive, silence descends over the winter trees. Beneath their bark, inside their twigs and branches, or lying among their fallen leaves under the snow, many lives await the coming of spring when the sap will rise again and the tale of *Once Upon a Tree* will be retold as it has been for millions of years.

The leafless hackberry tree adds interesting contrast to the winter landscape as it awaits the warmth of spring.

# GLOSSARY

Words in this glossary are derived from different languages. The source languages for some of these words are indicated with the following abbreviations:

Gr. – Greek
L. – Latin
ME. – Middle English
Pv. – Peruvian

Alga (L. *alga,* seaweed; -e, plural): a simple plant without stems, roots, or leaves that usually lives in water.

Amino acids: nutrients produced by trees that are used to build proteins of plants and animals.

Anther (Gr. *anthos,* flower): the portion of the male stamen that contains pollen.

Arthropod (Gr. *arthron,* joint; *poda,* feet): a member of a group of animals that all have jointed legs. The group includes such animals as insects, spiders, mites, woodlice, pseudoscorpions, centipedes, and millipedes.

Caterpillar: an immature form or larva of a moth or butterfly.

Chlorophyll (Gr. *chloros,* green; *phyllon,* leaf): a green pigment found mainly in leaves that captures the energy of sunlight for photosynthesis.

Chrysalis (Gr. *chrysos,* gold; L. *-alis,* pertaining to): the stage of development between the larva and adult of a butterfly; the pupa of a butterfly.

Diapause (Gr. *diapausis,* pause): a state of arrested development.

Fungus (L. *fungus,* mushroom; fungi, plural): a plant form that lacks chlorophyll and obtains its nutrients from dead plants and animals.

Gall (ME. *galle,* sore spot): an abnormal growth on a plant that often results from the action of certain insects or mites.

Guanophore (Pv. *guano,* animal droppings; Gr. *phore,* to carry): a pigment cell containing crystals of guanine, a white, crystalline chemical found in guano.

HONEYDEW: partially digested tree sap that has quickly passed through the gut of a sap-sucking insect and that still retains many nutrients.

INQUILINE (L. *inquilinus,* a lodger): an insect that is not responsible for making a gall but that lives in a gall as a "guest" of the gall maker and helps itself to the abundant food provided by the gall.

LARVA (-e, plural): an immature insect that shows little resemblance to the adult of its species. If the adult has wings, these wings first form inside the body of the larva.

LICHEN: a plant made up of an alga and a fungus that live together in a cooperative association.

LIPOPHORE (Gr. *lipo,* fat; *phore,* to carry): a yellow pigment cell containing fat droplets.

MELANOPHORE (Gr. *melanos,* black; *phore,* to carry): a black pigment cell.

METAMORPHOSIS (Gr. *meta,* change; *morphe,* form; *-sis,* process of): a change in the form of an insect during its development.

MYCORRHIZA (Gr. *mykes,* fungus; *rhiza,* root; -e, plural): a root-like structure formed by the association of roots and fungal filaments.

NECTAR (Gr. *nektar,* drink of the gods): a sweet liquid that insects obtain from special glands on flowers and other plant parts.

NYMPH: an immature insect that usually resembles adults of its species. If the adult insect has wings, these wings first appear on the outer surface of the nymph's body.

OVARY (L. *ovum,* egg): the enlarged, basal portion of the female pistil in which seeds develop.

OVIPOSITOR (L. *ovum,* egg; *positum,* to place): the egg-laying organ of an insect.

OVULE (L. *ovum,* egg): the portion of a flower and pistil that develops into a seed following pollination.

PALYNOLOGY (Gr. *palynos,* fine dust; *logy,* study of): the study of pollen.

PETIOLE (L. *petiolus,* little stalk): the stalk attaching a leaf to a stem or twig.

PHEROMONE (Gr. *phero,* carry; L. *moneo,* inform): a substance given off by an animal that causes a specific behavioral response in other members of the same species.

PHOTOSYNTHESIS (Gr. *photo,* light; *syn,* together; *thesis,* an arranging): the process by which green chlorophyll uses light, carbon dioxide, and water to produce sugars and oxygen.

PISTIL (L. *pistillum,* pestle): the female part of a flower that unites with pollen and subsequently produces seed.

POLLEN (L. *pollen,* dust): the part of a flower and male stamen that unites with the pistil to produce seed.

POLLINATION: the transfer of male pollen to a female pistil.

PUPA (-e, plural): a stage of insect development between the larva and the adult.

STAMEN (L. *stamen,* thread): the male part of a flower that produces pollen.

STIGMA (L. *stigma,* spot): the tip of the female pistil that receives pollen.

# INDEX

A number in **bold type** indicates that an illustration of the subject is found on this page.

# C



# D



# E

# F



# G



# H



# I



# K



# L

# M

# N



# O



# P

## Q



## R



## S



## T